CHARLIE MESNA

NO ORDINARY DOG

**The Ultimate Guide to Dog Training, Learn
the Basics and Proven Practices
on the Best Ways to Train Your Dog**

Descrierea CIP a Bibliotecii Naționale a României
CHARLIE MESNA
   NO ORDINARY DOG. The Ultimate Guide to Dog Training, Learn the Basics and Proven Practices on the Best Ways to Train Your Dog / Charlie Mesna – Bucharest: Editura My Ebook, 2021
   ISBN

CHARLIE MESNA

NO ORDINARY DOG

**The Ultimate Guide to Dog Training, Learn
the Basics and Proven Practices
on the Best Ways to Train Your Dog**

My Ebook Publishing House
Bucharest, 2021

TABLE OF CONTENTS

INTRODUCTION

Getting a new puppy or adult dog is always an exciting time for the entire family. There is a good reason why dogs are known as man's best friend, and a loyal dog is more than just a pet as they becoming a beloved member of the family.

In order to achieve that level of love and companionship, however, it is important to start you need puppy or adult dog off on the right foot. A solid grounding in obedience and problem behavior avoidance is essential to making your dog, and you, happier and healthier.

"How does your dog sit when you tell him to and mine doesn't?", "How can your dog heel to you like that?", "Wow! He comes when you tell him to" - Sounds familiar? If it does, you need to invest some time into a little bit of basic dog training. Starting to train your dog from a young age is crucial as the first few months of his life is when you will have the greatest influence on him; this is where he is shaped into the dog he is going to be when he is all grown up.

The most basic of dog training is to get your dog to sit and come. Teaching him those commands are essential for him to learn. These commands are used for various different reasons, if you are in competition, if your dog jumps making him sit will immediately get him off and "come" is the all-important one. If you take your dog for a walk, you let him of the leash and you expect him to come back to you, not run around the park with you chasing after him shouting at him to "get here right this instance". That would be just downright embarrassing!

To teach your dog how to come requires only the most basic of techniques but a lot of repetition. The simplest way to get him to come is have a toy in one hand and a treat in the other, when you are in the house simply walk away from him, hold out the toy and excitingly call him to you, when he comes over give him a treat, always use the command for come that you are going to use in the future. Doing this several times a day is a great way to teach him, but remember to have lots of long breaks so he doesn't get bored and stop enjoying it, and don't forget the treats!

Getting him to sit could be slightly harder but again only requires basic dog training. When you have mastered the come command call him to you, place your hand on the end of his back and say "sit" while gently pushing down on his backside, when he sits his bottom down give him a treat and a lot of praise. If you want him to sit longer just delay giving him the treat and the praise, get him to sit but take your time bending down to him and feeding him his titbit.

Basic dog training is simple and very effective. It should also be fun for you and your dog, it doesn't have to be hours and hours each day just may be 5 minutes or so. Don't forget to reward your dog and yourself for all the "hard" work though!!

Let's start with a look at getting started on basic puppy training, from bringing the new addition home to making sure he is properly socialized and behaved.

Chapter 1

The Basic Commands

There are of course many reasons for owners to want a calm, obedient and faithful dog. For one thing, obedient and trained dogs are happier dogs, less likely to get into tussles with people or with other dogs. Another reason is that many communities require that the dogs living in their neighborhoods be well trained. This is especially true for many breeds thought to have aggression and behavior problems such as dog breeds like pit bulls and rottweilers for instance.

And of course, training your dog well will also make him or her much better family companion, especially in households where there are young children. Many studies have shown that properdog training makes a big impact when it comes to cutting down the number of dog bits and other behavior problems encountered by dog owning households.

When considering training your own dog, or having someone else help you train it, there are certain basic commands that must be mastered in order for a dog to be considered truly trained. These basic commands include:

❖ *Heel* - it is important that any dog learn to walk beside its owner on a loose lead, neither pulling ahead nor lagging behind

❖ *Respond to the word "No"* - the word no is one word that all dogs must learn. Training your dog to respond to this important word can save you a ton of trouble.

❖ *Sit* - Training your dog to sit on command is a vital part of any dog training program.

❖ *Stay* - A well trained dog should remain where his or her owner commands, so stay is a very important command in dog training.

❖ *Down* - Lying down on command is more than just a cute trick; it is a key component of any successful dog training program.

The basic obedience commands that every dog must know are - "Heel", "No", "Sit", "Stay", "Down" and "Off". These six commands form the basis of every basic obedience class, and it is vital that you and your dog master these basic commands.

These are the fundamentals, and it will be impossible to move onto other commands, or to correct problem behaviors, without having mastered the basics.

Heel

Let's start with the most basic command of all, the heel command. Teaching a dog to heel is the fundamental first step in teaching the dog to walk properly on the leash. The proper place for the dog to walk is at your side, neither lagging behind nor straining to get ahead.

If your dog begins to forge ahead on the lead, gently tug on the leash. This will cause the training collar to tighten and give the dog a gentle reminder to fall back into line. If the dog begins to lag behind, gently urge him forward. A lure or toy is a good tool for the dog that constantly lags behind.

Once the dog is consistently walking at your side, try to change your pace and encouraging the dog to match his pace with yours. It should always be the dog who adjusts his pace to you; you should never adjust your pace to meet the needs of the dog.

The word "No"

The word no is an important one for your dog to learn, and one you may be using a lot as training begins. It is important that the dog learn to respond to a sharp "No" promptly and obediently.

The "Sit" command

The sit command is another vital link in the chain that is dog training. Teaching a dog to sit on command, using voice commands alone, will form the groundwork of much future training, so it is important for the dog to master this vital skill.

The sit command can be combined with the heel command. As you walk alongside your dog, stop abruptly. If your dog does not stop when you do, give a sharp tug on the leash to remind the dog. Many dogs will instinctively stop when you do, while others need to be reminded through the use of the leash and the training collar.

Once the dog has stopped by your side, urge him to sit by pushing gently on his hindquarters. It is important not to use too much pressure, or to push him down abruptly. Doing so could frighten, or even injure the dog. Rather, apply a steady downward pressure. Most dogs will recognize this as a sit command. It is important to say the word sit as you do this.

Repeat this procedure a few times by walking, stopping and sitting your dog. After a few repetitions, the dog will probably begin to sit down on his own every time he stops. It is important to say the word sit each time, so that the dog will eventually learn to respond to voicecommands alone.

The "Stay" command

Like the sit command, the stay command is a vital building block to other, more advanced training. For instance, the stay command is vital to teaching the dog to come when called, whichis in turn vital to off leash work.

The stay command can be made into an extension of the sit command. Have your dog sit, and while he is sitting, slowly back away. If the dog begins to follow you, as he probably will it first, come back to the dog and ask him to sit again. Repeat the process until you can reach the end ofthe leash without your dog getting up from a sitting position.

After the dog is reliably staying where you indicate, you can try dropping the leash and backing further away. It will probably take the dog some time to reliably stay where he is put without becoming distracted.

The "Down" command

The down command is another important part of any basic obedience training program. Teaching a dog to lie down on command is much more than an entertaining trick. The down command is very important in regaining control of a dog, or stopping a dog who is engaged in aninappropriate behavior.

The "Off" command

The off command is just as vital to as the other commands, and it forms the basis for latertraining, especially when training the dog not to chase people, cars, bikes, cats, etc.

For instance, when training a dog to remain still when a bicycle goes by, the owner would stand with the dog calmly on the leash. If the dog begins to strain against the leash, the owner sharply issues an "Off" command accompanied by a tug of the leash. Eventually the dog will learn to respond to the voice command alone.

Dog training does much more than just to create an obedient, willing companion. Training your dog properly actually strengthens the bond that already exists between dog and handler. Dogs are pack animals, and they look to their pack leader to tell them what to do. The key to successful dog training is to set you up as that pack leader.

Establishing yourself as pack leader is a very important concept for any potential dog trainer to understand. There is only one leader in every pack of dogs, and the owner must establish him or herself as the dominant animal. Failure to do so leads to all manner of behavior problems.

A properly trained dog will respond properly to all the owner's commands, and will not display anxiety, displeasure or confusion. A good dog training program will focus on allowing the dog to learn just what is expected of it, and will use positive reinforcement to reward desired behaviors.

In addition to making the dog a good member of the community, obedience training is a great way to fulfill some of the dog's own needs, including the need for exercise, the security that comes with knowing what is expected of it, a feeling of accomplishment and a good working relationship with its handler. Dog training gives the dog an important job to do, and an important goal to reach.

Giving the dog a job is more important than you may think. Dogs were originally bred by humans to do important work, such as herding sheep, guarding property and protecting people. Many dogs today have no important job to do, and this can often lead to boredom and neurotic behavior.

Basic obedience training, and ongoing training sessions, provides the dog with an important job to do. This is especially important for high energy breeds like German shepherds and border collies. Training sessions are a great way for these high energy dogs to use up their extra energy and simply to enjoy themselves.

Incorporating playtime into your dog training sessions is a great way to prevent both yourself and your dog from becoming bored. Always remember to play with your dog helps to strengthen the all-important bond between you as the pack leader and your dog.

Chapter 2

Training Your New Puppy

Bringing a new puppy into the household is always an exciting and fun time. Everyone wants to play with, cuddle and hold the little ball of fur. The last thing on the minds of most new puppy owners is training the new addition, but it is important that puppy training and socialization begin as early as possible.

In some ways training a puppy is easier than training an adult or adolescent dog. One reason is that the puppy is essentially a "blank slate", untroubled by past training techniques and other issues. In other ways, however, the puppy can be more difficult to train than an older dog.

One challenge to training a new puppy is that puppies are more easily distractible than adolescent and adult dogs. Everything is new to a puppy, and every new experience provides a new chance for distraction. For this reason, it is best to keep training sessions short when working with a puppy, and to end each training sessions on a positive note.

Socializing a new puppy is a vital part of any training program, and it is important for socialization to begin early. The window for socialization is very short, and a puppy that is not properly socialized to people, dogs and other animals by the time he or she is four months old often never develops the socialization he or she needs to become a good canine citizen.

Socialization training is vital to making your new puppy a good canine citizen, as dog aggression is a growing problem in many areas. A properly socialized dog learns how to play properly with other dogs, and overly aggressive play is punished by the other dogs in the play group.

This type of play learning is something that happens among siblings in litters of puppies. As the puppies play with each other, they learn what is appropriate and what is not.

Inappropriate behavior, such as hard biting or scratching, is punished by the other puppies, by the mother dog, or both.

Unfortunately, many puppies are removed from their mothers and sold or adopted before this socialization has fully occurred. Therefore, puppy play sessions are a very important part of any puppy training session. Most good puppy preschool training programs provide time in each session for this type of dog interaction.

Introducing your puppy to new experiences and new locations is also an important part of puppy training. Teaching your dog to be obedient and responsive, even in the face of many distractions, is very important when training dogs and puppies.

One great way to socialize your puppy both to new people and new dogs is to take it on a trip to your local pet store. Many major pet store chains, and some independent ones as well, allow pet parents to bring their furry children, and these stores can be great places for puppies to get used to new sights, sounds and smells. Of course you will want to make sure the store allows pets before heading over.

Learning how to interact with other dogs is something that normally would occur between littermates. However, since most dogs are removed from their mothers so soon, this littermate socialization often does not finish properly.

One vital lesson puppies learn from their littermates and from the mother dog is how to bite, and how not to bite. Puppies naturally roughhouse with each other, and their thick skin protects them from most bites. However, when one puppy bites too hard, the other puppies, or the mother dog, quickly reprimand him, often by holding him by the scruff of his neck until he submits.

The best way to socialize your puppy is to have it play with lots of other puppies. It is also fine for the puppy to play with a few adult dogs, as long as they are friendly and well socialized.

Many communities have puppy playschool and puppy kindergarten classes. These classes can be a great way to socialize any puppy, and for handler and puppy alike to learn some basic obedience skills.

When socializing puppies, it is best to let them play on their own and work out their own issues when it comes to appropriate roughness of play. The only time the owners should step in is if one puppy is hurting another, or if a serious fight breaks out. Other than that the owners should simply stand back and watch their puppies interact.

While this socialization is taking place, the pack hierarchy should quickly become apparent. Some puppies are ultra-submissive, rolling on their backs and baring their throats at the slightest provocation. Other puppies in the class will be dominant, ordering the other puppies around and telling them what to do. Watching the puppies play, and determining what type of personality traits your puppy has, will be very valuable in determining the best way to proceed with more advanced training.

As the socialization process proceeds, of course, it will be necessary to introduce the puppy to all sorts of humans as well as all sorts of puppies. Fortunately, the puppy kindergarten class makes this process quite easy, since every puppy gets to interact with every human. It is important that the puppy be exposed to men, and women, old people and children, black people and white people. Dogs do not see every human as the same. To a dog, a man and a woman are completely different animals.

It is also important to introduce the puppy to a variety of other animals, especially in a multi pet household. Introducing the puppy to friendly cats is important, as are introductions to other animals the puppy may encounter, such as rabbits, guinea pigs and the like. If your household contains a more exotic creature, it is important to introduce the puppy to it as early as possible, but to do it in a way that is safe for both animals.

It is often best to start by introducing the puppy to the smell of the other animal. This can be easily accomplished by placing a piece of the animals bedding, like a towel or bed liner, near where the puppy sleeps. Once the puppy is accustomed to the smell of the other creature, he or she is much more likely to accept the animal as just another member of the family.

It is important for puppy owners to structure their pet's environment so that the puppy is rewarded for good behaviors and not rewarded for others. One good example of this is jumping on people. Many people inadvertently reward this behavior because it can be cute. While it is true that jumping can be cute for a 10 pound puppy, it will not be so cute when that puppy has grown into a 100 pound dog.

Instead of rewarding the puppy for jumping, try rewarding it for sitting instead. This type of positive reinforcement will result in a well behaved adult dog that is a valued member of boththe family and the community at large.

This type of reinforcement can also be used in potty training the new puppy. For instance, teaching a puppy to use a unique surface such as gravel or asphalt is a good technique. The theory is that the puppy will associate this surface with going potty, and therefore be reluctantto use other surfaces (like your kitchen carpet for instance) as a potty.

It is best to introduce a new puppy to the household when everyone in the family is present, and when the household is as calm as possible. That is why animal care experts discourage parents from giving puppies and kittens as holiday presents. The holiday season is typically much too busy, with far too many distractions, for a young puppy or kitten to get the attention it needs. It is best to wait until the holidays have passed before introducing the new family member.

Once the puppy is part of the household, there are some things he or she will need to learn. One of the first challenges of a multi-story home will be learning to climb up and down the stair.

Many puppies are afraid of stairs, and that usually means that they do not know how to climb them properly. It is important for the puppy's owner to slowly build the confidence of the dog, starting off at the bottom of the stairs. In general, a wide stairway will probably be less frightening to the puppy.

To build confidence, the owner should go up the first step, and then encourage the puppy to join them, using their voice, treats or a toy. After the puppy has joined you on the first stair, go back down and repeat the process until the puppy will go up that step on his own. It is important to build confidence slowly and not rush the process. Taking a one step at a time approach is the best way to teach the puppy to not be afraid of stairs.

Another thing every new puppy must learn is how to accept the collar. Learning to wear a collar is important to every dog, but many puppies are baffled, frightened and bewildered by this new piece of equipment. Many puppies constantly try to remove their new collar by pawing and pulling at it.

Fit is important when choosing a collar for your new puppy. A properly fitted collar, chosen for your puppy's size, is more likely to be comfortable and accepted. While choke, slip and training collars can be good training aids, they should never be used as a substitute for a sturdy buckle type collar. And of course that collar should have an identification tag and license attached. This identification will be vital in having your puppy returned if she becomes separated from you.

The best way to introduce the puppy to the collar is to simply put the collar on and allow her to squirm, jump, roll and paw at the color to her heart's content. It is important to not encourage this behavior by trying to soothe the puppy, but it is just as important not to punish or reprimand the puppy.

The best strategy is to simply ignore the puppy and them her work through her issues with the collar on her own. Introducing distractions, such as food, toys or playing, is a good way to get the puppy used to the color. Getting the puppy to play, eat and drink while wearing the collar is a great way to get her used to it. After a few days, most puppies will not even know they are wearing a collar.

Teaching Your Puppy Proper Socialization Skills

Teaching a puppy or a dog with proper socialization skills is vital to the safety of both your dog between other dogs and people with whom he comes into contact. A properly socialized dog is a happy dog, and a joy to be around for both humans and animals. A poorly socialized dog or one with no socialization at all, is a danger to other animals, other people and even his own family.

Socialization is best done when the puppy is as young as possible the socialization lessons a young puppy learns are difficult to undo, and it is important to remember that the socialization skills the puppy learns will affect his behavior for the rest of his life.

A dog that is properly socialized will be neither frightened of nor aggressive towards either animals or humans. A properly socialized dog will take each new experience and stimulus in stride, and not become fearful or aggressive. Dogs that are not properly socialized often bite because of fear, and such a dog can become a hazard and a liability to the family who owns it. Improperly socialized dogs are also unable to adapt to new situations. A routine matter like a trip to the vets or to a friend's house can quickly stress the dog out and lead to all sorts of problems.

Socialization is best done when the puppy is very young, perhaps around 12 weeks of age. Even after 12 weeks, however, it is important that the puppy continues its socialization in order to refine the all-important social skills. It is possible to socialize an older puppy, but it is very difficult to achieve after the all-important 12 week period has passed.

There are so definite do's and don'ts when it comes to properly socializing any puppy. Let's startwith what to do. Later in this article we will explore what to avoid.

Socialization do's

❖ Make each of the socialization events as pleasant and non-threatening for the puppy as possible. If a puppy's first experience with any new experience is an unpleasant one, it will be very difficult to undo that in the puppy's mind. In some cases, an early trauma can morph into a phobia that can last for a lifetime. It is better to take things slow and avoid having the puppy become frightened or injured.

❖ Try inviting your friends over to meet the new puppy. It is important to included as many different people as possible in the puppy's circle of acquaintances, including men, women, children, adults, as well as people of many diverse ethnic backgrounds and ages.

❖ Also invite friendly and healthy dogs and puppies over to meet your puppy. It is importantfor the puppy to meet a wide variety of other animals, including cats, hamsters, rabbits and other animals he is likely to meet. It is of course important to make sure that all animals the puppy comes into contact with have received all necessary vaccinations.

❖ Take the puppy to many different places, including shopping centers, pet stores, parks, school playgrounds and on walks around the neighborhood. Try to expose the puppy to places where they will be crowds of people and lots of diverse activity going on.

❖ Take the puppy for frequent short rides in the car. During these rides, be sure to stop the car once in a while and let the puppy look out the window at the world outside.

❖ Introduce your puppy to a variety of items that may be unfamiliar. The puppy should be exposed to common items like bags, boxes, vacuum cleaners, umbrellas, hats, etc. that may be frightening to him. Allow and encourage the puppy to explore these items and see that he has nothing to fear from them.

❖ Get the puppy used to a variety of objects by rearranging familiar ones. Simply placing a chair upside down, or placing a table on its side, creates an object that your puppy will perceiveas totally new.

❖ Get the puppy used to common procedures like being brushed, bathed, having the nails clipped, teeth cleaned, ears cleaned, etc. Your groomer and your veterinarian with thank you forthis.

❖ Introduce the puppy to common things around the house, such as stairs. Also introduce the puppy to the collar and leash, so he will be comfortable with these items.

There are of course some things to avoid when socializing a puppy. These socialization don'tsinclude:

❖ Do not place the puppy on the ground when strange animals are present. An attack, or even a surprise inspection, by an unknown animal could traumatize the puppy and hurt his socialization.

❖ Do not inadvertently reward fear based behavior. When the puppy shows fear, it is normalto try to sooth it, but this could reinforce the fear based behavior and make it worse. Since biting is often a fear based behavior, reinforcing fear can create problems with biting.

- ❖ Do not force or rush the socialization process. It is important to allow the puppy to socialize at his own pace.

- ❖ Do not try to do too much too soon. Young puppies have short attention spans, and continuing lessons after that attention span has passed will be a waste of your time and yourpuppy's.

- ❖ Do not wait too long to begin. There is a short window in which to begin the socialization process. A young puppy is a blank slate, and it is important to fill that slate with positive socialization skills as early as possible.

Chapter 3

Leash/Collar Training

There are many different styles of dog training, and finding the one that works best for you is important for creating a dog that is a talented, loyal and faithful member of the family. All successful methods of dog training work to reinforce the relationship between dog and handler, and the foundation of any successful training program is getting the respect of the dog.

Fortunately, dogs are wired by nature to seek out leaders, and to follow the direction of those leaders.

Both leash/collar training and reward training have been around for a very long time, and they have proven their effectiveness over time. The type of training that works best will vary from dog to dog, and from breed to breed. It is important to remember that each breed of dog has its own unique qualities, reinforced by hundreds of years of selective breeding.

Of course personalities of individual dogs vary quite a bit, even within established breeds. You, as the owner of the dog, know better than anyone about which style of dog training will work best, so it is important to work with the trainer you choose to achieve your goal of a willing, obedient and friendly dog.

Leash and collar training is the best way to accomplish many types of dog training, particularly in situations where the dog must have a high level of reliability. For instance, dogs that have an important job to do, such as rescue dogs, police dogs and guard dogs, generally benefit from leash and collar training.

In leash and collar training, varying degrees of force can be used, ranging from slight prompts with the lead to very harsh corrections. The amount of correction used should be appropriate to the situation, since using too much correction, or too little, will be ineffective.

In a collar and leash based dog training program, first the dog is taught a particular behavior, generally with the leash. After the dog has demonstrated that it understands the command, the leash is then used to correct the dog if it disobeys, or when it makes a mistake. The leash is the main form of controlling and communicating with the dog in leash and collar training.

When using leash and collar training, the dog must be trained to trust the handler and accept his or her directions without question. In order for the dog to be fully trained, the handler must demonstrate the ability to place the dog into a posture or position he or she does not want to take. This does not mean using force, but it does generally require some level of physical manipulation. This manipulation is most easily and safely done using the main tool of leash and collar training – the leash.

It is important for every dog trainer to understand that the leash is simply a tool. While the leash is an important tool in this form of training, it is important for the dog trainer to be able to eventually achieve the same results using whatever tools are at hand.

Even when the only tools at hand are the owner's body and skill, the dog should be willing to obey. Creating a leader/follower relationship between handler and dog is still very important, and it is important to use the leash as a tool and not a crutch. A properly trained dog should be willing to obey whether the leash is present or not.

Training Your Dog with a Training Collar and Leash

The leash and training collar is the most basic piece of equipment used in training a dog. Using the lead and training collar properly is vital to successful dog training. The training collar is designed to apply a specific amount of pressure each

34

time the leash is tightened. The amount of pressure put on the leash controls the amount of pressure placed on the training collar, and the pressure can be adjusted according to how the dog responds.

How each dog responds to training with the leash and training collar is quite variable. Some dogs barely react the first time they encounter a collar and leash, while others fight this strange contraption with all their might. It is important to recognize how your own dog reacts, and to adapt your training program as needed.

The first part of training with collar and leash, of course, is to purchase a quality, well-made training collar that will fit your dog properly. There are many types of training collars and leashes on the market. The most important thing is to choose one that is sturdy and well made. The last thing you want to do is chase your dog down after he has broken his collar.

The length of the collar should be approximately two inches longer than the circumference of the dog's neck. It is important to accurately measure the dog's neck using a measuring tape. In order to get an accurate measurement, you must make sure that the tape is not tight around the dog's neck.

Most training collars come in even sizes, so you should round up to the next size if your dog's neck is an odd number. It is important that the chain that attaches to the collar be placed at the top of the dog's neck. That is where the training collar is designed to apply the best pressure.

The ability to apply varying degrees of pressure, and to relieve that pressure instantly, is what makes a training collar such an effective tool. It usually takes new users a little while to get used to using the training collar, and some styles of training collar require more finesse than others. If you are unsure which collar to choose, be sure to ask a professional dog trainer, or the management staff at your local pet store, for help.

After you have become familiar with the way the training collar works, it is time to begin using it to train your dog to walk properly on a lead. The well trained dog is one who will walk at his owner's side on a loose lead, neither dropping behind nor charging ahead.

The well trained dog will also vary his pace to meet that of his handler. Under no circumstances should the handler be forced to change his or her pace to match that of the dog.

If the dog does begin to charge ahead, it is important to correct the dog promptly by giving a quick tug on the leash. This will give the dog a good reminder that he needs to change his pace. It is important to quickly relieve the pressure as soon as the dog responds. The training collar is designed to relieve pressure as soon as the leash is loosened.

Most dogs will immediately respond to corrections by a good, properly used training collar. If the dog does not respond as directed, it may be necessary to apply greater pressure. This can be especially true of large dogs or those who have preexisting behavior or control problems. If you are still unable to get a response from your dog, it is possible that you are using a training collar that is not large enough for your dog. If you think this may be the case, be sure to ask for expert advice before proceeding.

Teaching a Puppy to Accept His Collar and Leash

Learning to walk on a collar and leash is the basis of all further training for every puppy. Until the puppy has learned to accept the collar and leash, it will be impossible to perform any additional training.

The first step toward getting the puppy to accept the collar and leash is to find a collar that fits the dog properly. It is important that the collar be neither too light nor too heavy, neither too thin nor too thick. A collar that is too light for the dog can be easily broken, while a collar that is too heavy may be uncomfortable for the puppy to wear. It is also important that the width of the color be appropriate for the size of the dog.

Determining the proper length of the collar is relatively easy. Simply wrap a tape measure or a string lightly around the dog's neck to get an accurate measurement. It is important that the tape measure not be tight, just slightly snug.

Most collars are sized in two inch increments, so you may have to round up to get a properly sized collar. For instance, if the dog has a 13" neck, you would buy a 14" collar, and so on.

After you have purchased the perfect collar, the next step is to put it on the dog and allow him to wear it around the house. Do not be dismayed if the dog whines, paws at the collar or otherwise tries to remove it. This is normal, and the dog should not be punished for it. It is best to simply ignore the dog and allow him to work out his own issues with the collar.

The dog should be allowed to wear the collar 24 hours a day for a number of days to get used to the feel of the collar on his neck. After the dog is accepting the collar well, it is time to start introducing the leash. A lightweight leash works best for this process.

Simply attach the leash to the dog's collar and allow him to walk around the house with it. The dog should of course be supervised during this process in order to make sure he does not get the leash caught on anything. Getting the leash caught or snagged could frighten the dog and create a leash phobia that will be hard to overcome.

In the beginning, the leash should only be attached for a few minutes at a time. It is important to attach the leash at happy times, such as playtime, meal time, etc. It is important for the dog to associate the leash with happy things. When the leash is not attached to the dog, it is a goodidea to keep it near the dog's food and water bowls. The dog should be encouraged to investigate the leash, and to discover that it is not something to fear.

After the dog is used to walking around with the leash attached, take the end of the leash in your hand and just hold it. Allow the dog to walk around. If the dog bumps into the end of theleash, just allow the dog to react and move as he desires. The goal of this exercise is to simplyallow the dog to get used to the feel of the collar and the leash.

It is important to allow the puppy plenty of time to get used to wearing the collar and leash before ever attempting to lead the puppy. It is best to perform this exercise in the home or other environment where the puppy feels safe and secure. After the puppy is comfortable and content walking on the leash in the home, it can slowly be taken outside. It is best to make these outside trips very short at the beginning, and to lengthen them slowly over time. Some puppies take to the collar and leash immediately, while others may require some additional time.

Training Your New Puppy to Accept the Collar and Lead

Walking on a collar and lead is an important skill that every dog must learn. Even the best trained dog should never be taken outside the home or yard without a sturdy collar and leash. Even if your dog is trained perfectly to go off lead, accidents and distractions do happen, and a collar, with proper identification attached, is the best way to be sure you will get your belovedcompanion back.

Of course before you can teach your new puppy to accept a leash, he or she must first learn to accept wearing a collar. The first step is to choose a collar that fits the dog properly. It is important to measure the puppy's neck, and to choose a collar size accordingly. After the collar has been put on the puppy, simply let him or her get used to it. It is not unusual for a puppy to try to pull on the collar, whine, roll or squirm when first introduced to a collar.

The best strategy is to simply ignore the puppy and let him or her get used to the collar. It is a mistake to either punish the dog for playing with the collar or to encourage the behavior.

40

Distracting the puppy often helps, and playing with a favorite toy, or eating some favorite treats, can help the puppy quickly forget that he or she is wearing this strange piece of equipment.

After the dog has learned to accept the collar, try adding the leash. Hook the leash to the collar and simply sit and watch the puppy. Obviously, this should only be done either in the house or in a confined outdoor area. The puppy should be allowed to drag the leash around on its own, but of course the owner should keep a close eye on the puppy to ensure that the leash does notbecome snagged or hung up on anything.

At first, the leash should only be left on for a few minutes at a time. It is a good idea to attach the leash at mealtimes, playtime and other positive times in the life of the puppy. That way thepuppy will begin to associate the leash with good things and look forward to it. If the puppy shows a high degree of fear of the leash, it is a good idea to place it next to the food bowl for awhile to let him get used to it slowly. Eventually, he will come to understand that the leash is nothing to be afraid of.

After the puppy is comfortable with walking around the house wearing the leash, it is time foryou to pick up the end of the leash for a few minutes. You should not try to walk the puppy on the leash; simply hold the end of the leash and follow the puppy around as he or she walks around. You should try to avoid situations where the leash becomes taut and any pulling or straining on the leash should be avoided. It is fine for the puppy to sit down. Try a few games with the collar and lead. For instance, back up and encourage the puppy to walk toward you. Don't drag the puppy forward, simply encourage him to come to you. If he does, praise him profusely and reward him with a food treat or toy. You should always strive to make all the time spent on the leash as pleasant as possible.

It is important to give the puppy plenty of practice in getting used to walking on the leash in the home. It is best to do plenty of work in the home, since it is a safe environment with few distractions. After the puppy is comfortable walking indoors on a leash, it is time to start going outside, beginning of course in a small, enclosed area like a fenced yard. After the puppy has mastered walking calmly outdoors on a leash, it is time to visit some places where there are more distractions. You may want to start with a place like a neighbor's yard. Walking your new puppy around the neighborhood is a good way to introduce your neighbors to the new puppy, while giving the puppy valuable experience in avoiding distractions and focusing on his leash training.

Puppies sometimes develop bad habits with their leashes, such as biting or chewing on the leash. To discourage this type of behavior, try applying a little bit of bitter apple, Tabasco sauce or similar substance (just make sure the substance you use is not toxic to dogs). This strategy usually convinces puppies that chewing the leash is a bad idea.

Training Your Dog to Not Pull On the Leash

Pulling on the leash is one of the most common misbehaviors seen on all kinds of dogs. Puppies and adult dogs alike can often be seen taking their owners for walks, instead of the other way around. Pulling on the leash can be much more than an annoying habit. Leash pulling can lead to escape in the case of a break in the collar or leash, and an out of control, off leash dog can be both destructive and dangerous to itself and to others.

Leash pulling can result from a variety of different things. In some cases, the dog may simply be so excited to go for a walk that he or she is unable to control themselves. In other cases, the dog sees itself as the leader of the pack, and he or she simply takes the "leadership position" at the front of the pack.

If excitement is the motivation for leash pulling, simply giving the dog a few minutes to calm down can often be a big help. Simply stand with the dog on the leash for a couple minutes and let the initial excitement of the upcoming walk pass. After the initial excitement has worn off, many dogs are willing to walk calmly on their leash.

If the problem is one of control, however, some retraining may be in order. All dog training starts with the owner establishing him or herself as the alpha dog, or pack leader, and without this basic respect and understanding, no effective training can occur. For dogs exhibiting these type of control issues, a step back to basic obedience commands is in order. These dogs can often be helped through a formal obedience school structure. The dog trainer will of course be sure to train the handler as well as the dog, and any good dog trainer will insist on working with the dog owner as well as the dog.

The basis of teaching the dog to walk calmly on the lead is teaching it to calmly accept the collar and lead. A dog that is bouncing up and down while the collar is being put on will not walk properly. Begin by asking your dog to sit down, and insisting that he sit still while the collar is put on. If the dog begins to get up, or gets up on his own after the collar is on, be sure to sit him back down immediately. Only begin the walk after the dog has sat calmly to have the collar put on, and continued to sit calmly as the leash is attached.

44

Once the leash is attached, it is important to make the dog walk calmly toward the door. If the dog jumps or surges ahead, gently correct him with a tug of the leash and return him to a sitting position. Make the dog stay and then move on again. Repeat this process until the dog is walking calmly by your side.

Repeat the above process when you reach the door. The dog should not be allowed to surge out of the door, or to pull you through the open door. If the dog begins this behavior, return the dog to the house and make him sit quietly until he can be trusted to walk through the door properly. Starting the walk in control is vital to creating a well-mannered dog.

As you begin your walk, it is vital to keep the attention of the dog focused on you at all times. Remember, the dog should look to you for guidance, not take the lead himself. When walking, it is important to stop often. Every time you stop, your dog should stop. Getting into the habit of asking your dog to sit down every time you stop is a good way to keep your dog's attention focused on you. Make sure your dog is looking at you, then move off again. If the dog begins to surge ahead, immediately stop and ask the dog to sit. Repeat this process until the dog is reliability staying at your side. Each time the dog does what you ask him to, be sure to reward him with a treat, a toy or just your praise.

Remember that if your dog pulls on the leash and you continue to walk him anyway, you are inadvertently rewarding that unwanted behavior. Dogs learn whether you are teaching them or not, and learning the wrong things now will make learning the right things later that much harder. It is important to be consistent in your expectations. Every time the dog begins to pull ahead, immediately stop and make the dog sit. Continue to have the dog sit quietly until his focus is solely on you. Then start out again, making sure to immediately stop moving if the dog surges ahead.

Taking Your Dog Training off Leash

Many dog owners are anxious to give their four legged companions the freedom of going off leash, but it is important not to rush that important step. Dogs should only be allowed off their leash after they have become masters of all the basic obedience commands, such as walking at your heel, sitting and staying on command

Another skill that must be completely mastered before the dog can be taken off the leash is the come when called command. Even if the dog can heel, sit and stay perfectly, if he cannot be relied upon to come when called, he is not ready to be taken off the leash.

Taking any dog off the leash, especially in a busy, crowded area, or one with a lot of traffic, is a big step and not one to be taken lightly. It is vital to adequately test your dog in a safe environment before taking him off his leash. After all, the leash is the main instrument of control. You must be absolutely certain you can rely on your voice commands for control before removing the leash.

After the dog has been trained to understand the sit, stay and come when called commands, it is important to challenge the dog with various distractions. It is a good idea to start by introducing other people, other animals, or both, while the dog is in a safe environment like a fenced in yard. Have a friend or neighbor stand just outside the fence while you hold your dog on the leash. As the friend or family member walks around the outside of the fence, watch your dog's reactions closely. If he starts to pull at the leash, quickly tug him back.

Repeat this exercise until the dog will reliably remain at your side. After this, you can try dropping the leash, and eventually removing the leash and repeating the distraction. It is important to vary the distractions, such as introducing other animals, other people, traffic,rolling balls, etc.

After your dog is able to remain still in the face of distraction, start introducing the come when called lessons with distractions in place. Try to invite some of the neighbors, and their dogs over to play with each other. As the dogs are playing in the fenced in yard, try calling your dog. When the dog comes to you, immediately give him lots of praise, and perhaps a food reward. After the dog has been rewarded, immediately allow him to go back to playing. Repeat this several times throughout the day, making sure each time to reward the dog and immediately allow him to go back to his fun.

After the dog has seemingly mastered coming when called in his own yard, try finding a local dog park or similar area where you can practice with your dog. It is important to make the area small, or to choose a fenced in area, in case you lose control of the dog. If you cannot find a fenced in area, choose an area well away from people and cars. Practice with your dog by allowing him to play with other dogs, or just to sniff around, then calling your dog. When he comes to you, immediately reward and praise him, then let him resume his previous activities. Doing this will teach the dog that coming to you is the best option and the one most likely to bring both rewards and continued good times.

Only after the dog has consistently demonstrated the ability to come when called, even when there are many distractions around, is it safe to allow him time off leash. Off leash time
48

should never be unsupervised time. It is important, both for your well-being and your dog's, which you know where, he is and what he is doing at all times. It is easy for a dog to get into trouble quickly, so you should always keep an eye on him, whether he is chasing squirrels in the park, playing with other dogs, or just chasing a ball with the neighbor's kids.

Chapter 4

Head Collar Training

The head collar has become an increasingly popular dog training tool in the past couple of years. Two of the most well-known brands of head collar on the market are the Gentle Leader and the Halti, but there are many other brands that incorporate the basic head collar concept.

Many people find the Gentle Leader easier to fit that the Halti, and in addition the Gentle Leader is designed to fasten around the dog's neck. The advantage of this design is that even if the dog is somehow able to wriggle out of the muzzle, it is still wearing a collar. This safety feature is very important, especially during training outside or in novel situations. On the other hand, the Halti offers better control of the dog, and for this reason it is often favored when working with very aggressive dogs.

Training a dog with a head collar has a number of advantages over training with a traditional or training collar. For one thing, head collars are often easier to use for beginning dog trainers than are training collars. Head collars are also quite effective at preventing dogs from pulling, or controlling and retraining dogs that tend to pull.

Head collars can also be quite effective at controlling dogs in difficult situations, such as controlling a dog that wants to be with other dogs. Most owners know of some situations in which their dogs are difficult to control, and head collars can be quite effective at controllingthese volatile situations.

Head collars can be excellent for controlling dogs that are very strong, or for working with a dog in an area that contains a great many distractions. For instance, head collars are great for whenyour dog is on an outing, or in an area where there will be other dogs and other distractions.

Even though a head collar can be a great tool, it should not be used as a replacement for effective dog training. A head collar is most effective when it is used in combination with strong and sensible dog training methods, such as reward training and other forms of positive reinforcement.

Disadvantages of Head Collars

Even though head collars have many advantages, they have some distinct disadvantages as well. For one thing, head collars tend to make many dogs dependent on the equipment, and they quickly learn the difference between their regular collar and the head collar, and adjust their behavior accordingly.

In addition, some dogs, particularly those not accustomed to wearing a head collar, dislike wearing it and paw at it, try to rub it off or pull excessively. If your dog exhibits this behavior, the best strategy is to keep it moving until it learns to accept the collar. A good alternative is to have the dog sit by pulling up on the dog's head.

Another disadvantage of the head collar is the reaction that many people have to it. Many people think that a head collar is a muzzle, and react to the dog as if it may bite. While this is not necessarily a defect of the head collar, many people do find it troublesome.

Dog training with a head collar is much like training with a training collar or any other equipment. While the head collar can be an important and useful tool, it is important to use it appropriately, follow all package instructions, and to combine its use with solid training methods. The eventual goal of dog training with a head collar should be to have the dog behave as well with a regular collar as it does with the specialized head collar.

Chapter 5

Training Collar or Choke Collar

The basic dog training collar goes by many names, including choke collar, choke chain, training collar, correction collar and slip collar. These training collars are among the most popular and most commonly used tools with both amateur and professional dog trainers.

While a training collar is an effective tool, like any tool it must be used properly in order to be effective for you and safe for the dog. Among the most important considerations when using atraining collar are:

❖ *How the collar fits the dog.* It is essential that the training collar be properly fitted to the dog. A properly fitted training collar is easier to use and safer for the dog.

❖ *Putting the training collar on properly.* There is a right way and a wrong way to fit a training collar and putting it on wrong will make it both ineffective and potentially dangerous.

❖ *Using the collar properly.* A training collar should be used as a sharp reminder to the dog, not as punishment. It is important that constant pressure be avoided when using a training collar.

❖ *The weight of the chain and the size of the links on the training collar.* It is important that the weight of the chain be appropriate to the size and weight of the dog.

❖ *The placement of the collar on the dog.* It is important to properly place the collar on the dog.

The Importance of a Properly Fitted Training Collar

Determining if the training collar is the right size is relatively easy. The ideal size training collar should fit snugly, yet comfortably over the dog's head. It is important that the training collar not fit too tightly, but it should not be too loose either. A training collar that is too tight will be too hard to put on and off. On the other hand, a training collar that is too loose can accidentally fall off of the dog's head when it lowers its head.

It is also important to know that a training collar that is too long for the dog requires a great deal of finesse to use properly. A collar that is too long can still be used, but it will require more skill on the part of the handler.

Properly Sizing and Measure the Dog for a Training Collar

It is best to measure the dog's neck with a tape measure, and then add 2 to 3 inches to that measurement. So if your dog has a neck 12" in diameter, you would want to buy a training collar that is 14" in length. Chain slip collars are generally sized in two inch increments.

Fitting the Collar Properly

When fitting a training collar, the part of the chain which is connected to the leash should be on the top of the dog's neck. With this type of arrangement, the collar releases the instant the leash is loosened. Training collars work by making the collar tight and loose in a fast manner.

Tightening the collar is the first part of the correction, and making it loose is the second part of the correction.

If the part of the training collar that is attached to the leash is not on the top of the dog's neck, the collar can still be made tight, but it will not release back to a loose state easily.

This constant pressure on the dog's neck initiates a counter response on the part of the animal, and the dog will quickly learn to pull and strain against the leash.

Finally, it is important to purchase a training collar that is well made and strong. Buying a high quality training collar, slip collar or choke collar is vital to the safety of yourself and your dog.

If the worst happens, and your dog's training collar does break, it is important not to panic. Most dogs will be unaware that they have broken the collar, at least for a few minutes. In most cases, if you act as if the leash is still connected, you can probably get control of your dog back quickly.

When securing a loose dog, the best strategy is to make a quick slip lead by running the snap on the leash through its handle and then slipping it over the dog's head. It may not be the best arrangement, but it will certainly do in a pinch.

Chapter 6

Reward Training

Reward training is often seen as the most modern method of training a dog, but reward training is probably much older than other methods of dog training. It is possible that reward training for dogs has been around as long as there have been dogs to train. Early humans probably used some informal kind of reward training when taming the wolf pups that eventually evolved into modern dogs.

Many principles of modern reward training date back many decades. However, what is called reward training today has only enjoyed is remarkable popularity for the past 10 or 15 years.

Many reward training enthusiasts are less enthusiastic about other methods of dog training, such as the traditional leash and collar method. However, the best approach to training any individual dog is often a combination of leash/collar training and reward training.

In addition, a training method that works perfectly for one dog may be totally inappropriate for another, and vice versa. Some dogs respond wonderfully to reward training and not at all to leash and collar training, while others respond to leash/collar training and are not at all motivated by reward training. Most dogs fall somewhere in the middle of these two extremes.

Clicker training is one of the most popular forms of reward training these days. While clicker training is not the answer for every dog, it can be a remarkably effective method of training many dogs. In clicker training, the dog is taught to associate a clicking sound with a reward, like a treat. The trainer clicks the clicker when the dog does something good, followed immediately by a treat. Eventually, the dog learns to respond to the clicker alone.

Most reward training uses some sort of food reward, or a reward that is associated with getting food. In most cases, complex behaviors can only be taught using this kind of positive reinforcement, and you will find that the people who train dogs for movies and television use reward training almost exclusively.

Reward training is used in all forms of dog training, including police work and military applications. Most scent detection, tracking and police dogs are trained using some form of reward training. Reward training is also a very effective way to teach many basic obedience commands.

Reward training often incorporates the use of a lure in order to get the dog into the position desired by the trainer. The lure is used to get the dog to perform the desired behavior on his or her own and of his or her own free will.

It makes a great deal of sense to get the dog to perform the desired behavior without any physical intervention on the part of the handler. Getting the dog to perform a behavior without being touched is important.

After the dog has performed the desired behavior, it is given a reward, also called a positive reinforcement. Treats are often used as reinforcers, but praise, such as "good dog" or a pat on the head, can also be effective rewards.

Making a dog that has been reward trained a reliable dog is important, especially when the dog has an important job, like police work or drug detection, to do. For that reason it is important to get the dog accustomed to working around distractions, and to properly socialize the animal to both people and other animals.

Many dog trainers make the mistake of only training the dog inside the house or back yard, and only when the handler is there. In order to become a reliably trained companion, the dog must be taken outside the confines of its safety zone and introduced to novel situations.

It is also important to teach the dog to pay attention to the handler at all times. By having the attention from the dog means having control of the dog. Reward training is very effective at getting the respect and the attention of the dog when used properly.

Treats and Food Based Rewards

Training with treats and other food based rewards is a great way to motivate your dog and speed the training process along. Most dogs are highly motivated by food rewards, and treat training using this kind of positive reinforcement is used to train all sorts of animals, including tigers, lions, and elephants and even house cats.

Before you begin a treat based training session, however, it is a good idea to test the dog to make sure that food will motivate him through the session. Begin around the dog's regular meal time by taking a piece of its food and waving it in front of the dog's nose. If the dog shows an enthusiasm for the food, now is a great time to start the training. If the dog shows little interest or none at all, it may be best to put off the training until another time. Don't be afraid to delay the start of meal time in order to pique the dog's interest in training. The advantages of proper training will far outweigh any delay in feeding.

It is generally best to get the dog used to regular feedings, instead of leaving food out all the time. Not only does free feeding encourage the dog to overeat and increase the chances of obesity, but a free fed dog may never be fully motivated in reward based training.

The Come When Called Command

Once your dog has shown interest in the food offered to it, it is time to begin the training. Since you already got your dogs undivided attention by showing it food, now is a great time to start. Give the dog a few pieces of food right away, and then back up a few steps. While holding the food in your hand, so "come here". When the dog comes to you, praise him effusively and give him a few pieces of food.

After the dog is coming to you easily, add a sit command and hold the collar before you give the food. After the sit command is mastered, other commands, and even some tricks, can be added.

Food based positive reinforcement training is the best way to teach a variety of importantbehaviors.

One good exercise is the sit command, stay, come when called exercise. This exercise can begin with the owner walking the dog, then stopping and asking the dog to sit. After the dog is sitting quietly, the owner backs away and asks the dog to stay. Ideally the dog should continue to stay until called by the owner, even if the leash is dropped. At the end of the exercise, the owner calls the dog. When the dog comes to the owner, it receives food and praise from the owner.

This exercise should be repeated several times, until the dog is reliably coming when called.

It is important to keep the training sessions short, especially in the beginning, to keep the dog from becoming bored, and from consuming its entire meal in the form of treats. After the dog has been responding regularly, the treats and food rewards can be slowly reduced. It is important to still provide these food rewards, but it may no longer be necessary to provide as many. After a while, as well, it will not be necessary to give the dog treats every single time he responds as requested. In general, it should only be necessary for the dog to receive a food treatone out of every five times he comes on demand. The other four successes can be rewarded with praise and scratches.

Once the dog understands the basics of the "come here" exercise, the basic exercise can be expanded, and many games can be created. These types of games can be great fun for owner and dog alike, as well as a great learning experience. Some off leash work can be introduced as well, but it is always best to start with the dog in a safe environment, such as a fenced back yard. For variety, you can try taking the dog to other safe environments, such as a friend's house, a neighbor's fenced yard or a local dog park. Try turning the dog loose in these safe places, and practice the come when called exercise. Always praise the dog extensively, scratch him behind the ears and tell him what a good dog he is. The goal should be to make coming to the owner a more pleasant experience than whatever the dog was doing before he was called.

Using Positive Reinforcement

Training dogs using positive reinforcement and reward training has long been recognized as both highly effective for the owner and a positive experience for the dog. Positive reinforcement training is so important that it is the only method used to train dangerous animals like lions and tigers for work in circuses and in the movie and television industry. Proponents of positive reinforcement swear by the effectiveness of their techniques, and it is true that the vast majority of dogs respond well to these training methods.

One reason that positive reinforcement training is so effective is that is uses rewards to teach the dog what is expected of it. When the dog performs the desired behavior, he is provided with a reward, most often in the form of a food treat, but it could be a scratch behind the ears, a rub under the chin or a pat on the head as well. The important thing is that the dog is rewarded consistently for doing the right thing.

Reward training has become increasingly popular in recent years, but chances are some sort of reward training between humans and dogs has been going on for hundreds if not thousands of years.

When understanding what makes reward training so effective, some knowledge of the history of humans and dogs is very helpful. The earliest dogs were probably wolf pups that were tamed and used by early humans for protection from predators, as alarm systems and later for guarding and herding livestock. It is possible that the wolf pups that made the best companions were the most easily trained, or it is possible that these early dogs were orphaned or abandoned wolf pups. Whatever their origin, there is little doubt today that the vast variety of dogs we see today have their origin in the humble wolf.

Wolf packs, like packs of wild dogs, operate on a strict pack hierarchy. Since wolf and dog packs hunt as a group, this type of hierarchy, and the cooperation it brings, is essential to the survival of the species. Every dog in the pack knows his or her place in the pack, and except in the event of death or injury, the hierarchy, once established, rarely changes.

Every dog, therefore, is hard wired by nature to look to the pack leader for guidance. The basis of all good dog training, including reward based training, is for the handler to set him or herself up as the pack leader. The pack leader is more than just the dominant dog, or the one who tells all the subordinates what to do. More importantly, the pack leader provides leadership and protection, and his or her leadership is vital to the success and survival of the pack.

It is important for the dog to see itself as part of a pack, to recognize the human as the leader of that pack, and to respect his or her authority. Some dogs are much easier to dominate than others. If you watch a group of puppies playing for a little while, you will quickly recognize the dominant and submissive personalities.

A dog with a more submissive personality will generally be easier to train using positive reinforcement, since he or she will not want to challenge the handler for leadership. Even dominant dogs, however, respond very well to positive reinforcement. There are, in fact, few dogs that do not respond well to positive reinforcement, also known as reward training.

Positive reinforcement is also the best way to retrain a dog that has behavior problems, especially one that has been abused in the past. Getting the respect and trust of an abused dog can be very difficult, and positive reinforcement is better than any other training method at creating this important bond.

No matter what type of dog you are working with, chances are it can be helped with positive reinforcement training methods. Based training methods on respect and trust, rather than on intimidation and fear, is the best way to get the most from any dog.

Chapter 7

Crate and House Training

House training is one of the most important parts of training any dog to be a valued part of the family. As with many other aspects of dog training, the best way to house train a dog is to use the dog's own nature to your benefit.

The great thing about dogs, and the thing that can make house training much easier, is that dogs are instinctively very clean animals. Dogs would rather not soil the areas where they sleep and eat. In addition, dogs are very good at developing habits regarding where they like to urinate and defecate. For example, dogs that are used to eliminating on concrete or gravel will prefer to eliminate there rather than on grass or dirt. It is possible to use these natural canine habits when house training your dog.

Setting Up the Training Area

The first step in house training your dog is to set up your training area. A small, confined space such as a bathroom, or part of a kitchen or garage, works best as a training area. This method of training differs from crate training. Crate training is great for puppies and small dogs, but many larger dogs find a crate too confining.

It is important for the owner to spend as much time in the training area with his or her dog as possible. It is important for the owner to play with the dog in the training area, and to let the dog eat and sleep in that area. The dog should be provided with a special bed in the training area, anything from a store bought bed to a large towel to a large box. At first, the dog may eliminate in this area, but once the dog has recognized it as his or her own space, he or she willbe reluctant to soil it.

After the dog has gotten used to sleeping in the bed, the owner can move it around the house, relocating it from room to room. When you are not with your dog, the dog should be confinedto the training area.

Setting Up the Toilet Area

The second part of house training is to set up the toilet area for the dog. It is important for the dog to have access to this place every time he or she needs to eliminate. It is also important forthe owner to accompany the dog each time until he or she gets into the habit of eliminating in the toilet area. This will ensure that the dog uses only the established toilet area.

A set feeding schedule makes the house training process a lot easier for both the owner and the dog. Feeding the dog on a regular basis will also create a regular schedule for the dog's toilet habits. Once you know when your dog is likely to need to eliminate, it will be simple to guide the dog to the established toilet area.

Once the dog has established a toilet area and is using it on a regular basis, it is very important to not confine the dog without access to the toilet area for long periods of time. That is because if the dog is unable to hold it, he or she may be forced to eliminate in the training area. This habit can make house training much more difficult.

Continuing the House Training Process

After the dog is consistently eliminating in the toilet area and not soiling the training area, it is time to extend that training area to the rest of the home. This process should be done slowly, starting with one room and slowly expanding to the rest of the house. The area should only be extended once you are sure of the dog's ability to control its bladder and bowels.

When you first expand the training area to a single room, let the dog eat, play and sleep in that room, but only when supervised. When it is not possible to supervise the dog, place it back in the original training area. Then, after the dog has accepted the room as an extension of the original training area, the area can be extended.

Speeding up the Process

If this process is too lengthy for your needs, it can be speeded up, but it is important to proceed cautiously. It is easier to take your time up front than to retrain a problem dog later. One way to successfully speed up house training is to praise and reward the dog each and every time it uses the established toilet area. It is also important not to punish the dog for mistakes. Punishment will only confuse the dog and slow down the house training process.

The Do's and Don'ts of House Training

House training a puppy is very important for the well-being of both the puppy and the owner. The number one reason that dogs are surrender to animal shelters is problems with inappropriate elimination, so it is easy to see why proper house training is such an important consideration.

It is important to establish proper toilet habits when the puppy is young, since these habits canlast a lifetime, and be very hard to break once they are established. It is very important for the owner to house break the puppy properly. In most cases, true house training cannot begin until the puppy is six months old. Puppies younger than this generally lack the bowel and bladder control that is needed for true house training.

Puppies younger than six months should be confined to a small, puppy proofed room when the owner cannot supervise them. The entire floor of the room should be covered with newspapers or similar absorbent materials, and the paper changed every time it is soiled. As the puppy gets older, the amount of paper used can be reduced as the puppy begins to establish a preferred toilet area. It is this preferred toilet area that will form the basis of later house training.

The Do's of House Training Your Puppy:

❖ Always provide the puppy with constant, unrestricted access to the established toilet area.

❖ When you are at home, take the puppy to the toilet area every 45 minutes.

❖ When you are not at home or cannot supervise the puppy, you must be sure the puppy cannot make a mistake. This means confining the puppy to a small area that has been thoroughly puppy proofed. Puppy proofing a room is very similar to baby proofing a room, since puppies chew on everything.

❖ Always provide a toilet area that does not resemble anything in your home. Training the puppy to eliminate on concrete, blacktop, grass or dirt is a good idea. The puppy should never be encouraged to eliminate on anything that resembles the hardwood flooring, tile or carpet he may encounter in a home.

❖ Praise and reward your puppy every time he eliminates in the established toilet area. The puppy must learn to associate toileting in the established areas with good things, like treats, toys and praise from his owner.

❖ Always keep a set schedule when feeding your puppy, and provide constant access to fresh, clean drinking water. A consistent feeding schedule equals a consistent toilet schedule.

❖ Using a crate can be a big help in helping a puppy develop self-control. The concept behind crate training is that the puppy will not want to toilet in his bed area.

❖ And finally, it is important to be patient when house training a puppy. House training can take as long as several months, but it is much easier to house train right the first time than to retrain a problem dog.

72

The Don'ts of House Training Your Puppy:

❖ Never reprimand or punish the puppy for mistakes. Punishing the puppy will only cause fear and confusion.

❖ Do not leave food out for the puppy all night long. Keep to a set feeding schedule in order to make the dog's toilet schedule as consistent as possible.

❖ Do not give the puppy the run of the house until he has been thoroughly house trained.

House training is not always the easiest thing to do, and some dogs tend to be much easier to house train than others. It is important, however to be patient, consistent and loving as you train your dog. A rushed, frightened or intimidated dog will not be able to learn the important lessons of house training. Once you have gained your puppy's love and respect, however, you will find that house training your puppy is easier than you ever expected.

Dealing with House Training Your Dog

House training is one of those issues that every dog owner must grapple with. In most cases house training is the first major milestone in the relationship between owner and dog, and it can sometimes be difficult and confusing for owner and dog alike.

The best house training procedures are those that use the dog's own instincts to the owner's advantage. These strategies take into account the dog's reluctance to soil the spots where he eats and sleeps. This is the concept behind den training and crate training. Dogs are very clean animals, and in nature they always avoid using their dens as toilet areas.

These kinds of natural training methods generally work very well, for both puppies and older dogs. Naturally, older, larger dogs will need a larger area for their den, and crate training is generally best used for puppies and small dogs.

When house training a dog or a puppy, however, it is important to pay close attention to the signals the dog is sending. It is also important to be consistent when it comes to feeding times, and to provide the dog with ready access to the toilet area you establish on a regular basis.

It is important as well to never try to rush the process of house training. While some dogs are naturally easier to train, most puppies and adult dogs will experience at least one or two slip ups during the house training process. When these accidents occur, it is important to not get mad and punish the dog. Accidents during house training usually mean that the owner is trying to move too fast, or that the dog has been left alone for too long. In this case, it is best to just take a step back and start the process again.

It is also important for the owner to reward the dog enthusiastically when it does its business in the appointed area. The dog should learn to associate doing its business in its toilet area with good things like treats, rewards and praise.

During the house training process, the den area starts out very small, often as small as half of a small room in the beginning. As the dog learns to control his bladder and bowels better, and the owner learns to anticipate the dog's toilet needs, the den area can be slowly expanded. It is important not to make the den area too large too soon. The den area must be expanded slowly in order for the house training process to move along smoothly.

It is important for the dog to be properly introduced to its den. Many dogs, particularly those who have never been confined before, such as those who have spent their lives as outdoor dogs, may react to the den area as if it is a prison, and constantly whine, cry and try to escape the den. It is important that the dog learn to accept its den as a home and not a cage.

One problem many dog owners overlook when house training a dog is that of boredom. Boredom is actually the root cause of many behavior problems in dogs, including chewing and other destructive behaviors. Boredom can also be the root cause of problems with house training.

Dogs that are bored often consume large amounts of water during the day, and this excess water consumption can lead to the need to urinate often, even in its den area. Since soiling the den area goes against the dog's nature, he can quickly become confused and frightened, thereby setting the house training program back even further.

To prevent the dog from becoming bored when you are away from home, be sure to provide him with lots of different kinds of toys, as well as a safe and secure place to sleep. In addition, a vigorous period of play time can help the dog sleep while you are away. In addition, playing with the dog in its den area will help him bond with this area and recognize it as a safe, secure home.

Dealing with House Training Issues

The best house training uses the dogs own instincts to avoid soiling its bed to train the dog where and where not to eliminate. That is the basis behind crate training, in which the dog is confined to its crate in the absence of the owner, and den training, in which the dog is confined to a small area of the home. In essence, the crate, or the room, becomes the dog's den.

Dogs are naturally very clean animals, and they try their best to avoid using their dens as toilets.

This type of training usually works very well, both for puppies and for older dogs. Problems with this type of toilet training are usually the result of not understanding the signals the dog is sending, not being consistent with feeding times, or trying to rush the process.

While the house training process can be sped up somewhat by consistently praising the dog and rewarding it for toileting in the proper place, some dogs cannot be rushed through this important process. It is always best to house train the dog properly the first time than to go back and retrain a problem dog.

If the dog continues to soil the den area after house training, the most likely reason is that the owner has left the dog in the den for too long. Another reason may be that the den area is too large. In this case, the best strategy is to make the den area smaller or to take the dog to the toilet area more frequently.

If the dog soils the bed that has been provided in the den area, it is most likely because the owner has left the dog there for too long, and the dog had an understandable accident. Or it could be that the dog has not yet adopted this area as the bed. In addition, urinary tract infections and other medical conditions can also cause dogs to soil their beds. It is important to have the dog thoroughly checked out by a veterinarian to rule out any medical problems.

One other reason for house training accidents that many people overlook is boredom. Dogs who are bored often drink large amounts of water and therefore must urinate more frequently than you might think. If you notice your dog consuming large amounts of water, be sure to take the dog to the established toilet area more often, and provide the dog with toys and other distractions to eliminate boredom.

Boredom is the root cause of many dog behavior problems, not only house training issues. Chewing and other destructive behaviors are also often caused by boredom and separation anxiety.

Other problems with house training can occur when the dog's den is not properly introduced. In some cases dogs can react to the den as if it is a prison or a punishment. Those dogs may exhibit signs of anxiety, such as whining, chewing and excessive barking. It is important for the dog to feel secure in its den, and to think of it as a home and not a cage.

The best way to house train a puppy or dog, or to re-house train a problem dog, is to make you aware of the dog's habits and needs. Creating a healthy, safe sleeping and play area for your dog, as well as a well-defined toilet area, is important for any house training program.

House training is not always an easy process, but it is certainly an important one. The number one reason that dogs are surrendered to animal shelters is problems with inappropriate elimination, so a well-structured house training program can literally be a lifesaver for your dog.

Crate Training for Dogs and Puppies

Crate training is one of the most effective ways of house breaking any puppy or dog. Crate training is very efficient, and very effective, since it uses the natural instinct of the dog to achieve the desired result of a clean house and a well-trained dog.

The concept behind crate training is that a dog naturally strives to avoid soiling the area where it eats and sleeps. By placing the dog in the crate, this instinct is enhanced. The dog will come to see the crate as its den, and it will try to avoid soiling its den.

The key to successful crate training for a puppy or an older dog, as with other forms of dog training, is to establish a good routine. This routine will enhance the ability of the dog to do its business in the right place, and avoid eliminating in the wrong place. It is important to shower the dog with praise each and every time it eliminates in the established toilet area, and not to express frustration or anger when the dog makes a mistake.

It is important to confine the dog or puppy to a small part of the house, generally one puppy proofed room, when you are not at home. The room should contain a soft bed, fresh water and some favorite toys to prevent the dog from becoming bored and frustrated.

Crate training is different from confining the dog to one room, however. With crate training, the puppy or dog is confined to a crate when unsupervised. The idea is that the dog will think of this crate as its home, and not want to soil is home.

When crate training, it is important to remove the dog from the crate as soon as possible after returning home, and to take the dog promptly to the previously established toilet area. When the dog does its business in this toilet area, be sure to provide lots of praise and treats. It is important that the dog learn to associate proper toilet procedures with good things like treats and toys.

It is important to never leave the dog in its crate for long periods of time, as this will confuse the dog and force it to soil its sleeping area. The crate is simply a tool, and it should not be abused by leaving the dog in it for extended periods of time. If the dog is left in the crate for too long, it could set back the training program by weeks if not months.

The dog should only be confined to the crate when you are at home. During day time except during the night time, dog should be given the opportunity to relieve itself every 45 minutes or so. Each time the dog is taken out; it should be put on a leash and immediately taken outside. Once outside the house, the dog should be given three to five minutes to do its business. If the dog does not eliminate in this time period, it should be immediately returned to the crate.

If the dog does its business during the set time period, it should be rewarded with praise, food, play, affection and either an extended walk or a period of play inside or outside the home.

During the crate training period, it is important to keep a daily diary of when the dog does its business each day. If the dog is on a regular feeding schedule, the toilet schedule should be consistent as well. Having a good idea of when the dog needs to eliminate each day will be a big help during the house training process. After the dog has used his established toilet area, you will be able to give the dog free run of the house to play and enjoy him.

Dealing with Accidents during Crate Training

It is very important to not punish the puppy or dog when it makes a mistake or has an accident during the crate training process. If there has been an accident, simply clean it up. Accidents during house training mean that you have provided the dog with unsupervised access to the house too quickly. The dog should not be allowed unsupervised access to the home until you can trust her bowel and bladder habits. If mistakes do occur, it is best to go back to crate training. Taking a couple of steps back will help move the house training process along, while moving too quickly could set things back.

Chapter 8

Dog Obedience Training

Obedience training is one of the most important and most effective things any owner can do for his or her dog. A properly obedience trained dog is a happy, productive and safe member of the family, while a untrained dog can be destructive and even dangerous.

Dogs are designed by nature to follow leaders, and to look for that leadership. As pack animals, dogs naturally follow the directions of their pack leader. In the absence of a strong leader, the dog may assume this role itself. Dogs that think of themselves as the leader of their human pack can become uncooperative, destructive and even dangerous.

Proper obedience training opens up important lines of communication between handler and dog. The basis of any obedience training program is to gain the cooperation and respect of the animal. This respect cannot be exerted through rough handling methods or mistreatment. It must instead be earned through leadership and proper training techniques.

Basic obedience training consists of teaching the dog what to do and what not to do. When it comes to desired behaviors, it is important for the dog to learn and respond to basic commands, such as heeling when walking, stopping on command, sitting when directed, coming when called and staying where the handler directs.

The list of what not to do is also important when it comes to obedience training. Some of the don'ts of obedience training include – not jumping up on people, not forging ahead when walking and, not chewing the furniture or your property, and not getting out of control whenexposed to novel situations.

In essence, obedience training involves establishing the social hierarchy that is so important to dogs as pack animals. When your dog follows your obedience commands, such as – come, stay, sit, heel, etc., he or she is showing compliance and submissiveness. This is the same type of behavior a submissive member of a wild dog pack would show to the alpha dog in that pack.

As with any type of dog training, it is important that obedience training sessions be fun and rewarding for both dog
84

and handler. A happy, healthy dog will be best able to learn, and keeping the dog happy during the training sessions will make life easier for both yourself and your dog. Obedience training has many benefits for the dog as well as the handler. For one thing, a well-trained, obedient dog can be permitted a larger amount of freedom than an untrained dog. For instance, a dog that has been properly trained to come when called can safely enjoy some off leash play time at the local park.

There is always a debate over whether it is easier to obedience train puppies or older dogs. The fact is that both puppies and older dogs can be successfully trained to be willing, obedient companions. It is generally easier to train puppies and young dogs than it is to retrain dogs that have developed behavior problems. Even problem dogs, however, can be successfully retrained using basic obedience training and control concepts.

When obedience training puppies, however, it is important to remember that puppies generally have a shorter attention span than to do full grown dogs. It is important, therefore to keep training sessions short in the beginning. It is also important to incorporate lots of play with other puppies, dogs and other animals, as well as lots of different people. Proper socialization is very important to creating a safe, healthy and happy companion dog.

There are many obedience training classes held in all parts of the country, and new puppy anddog owners are encouraged to enroll in one of these classes. Not only do puppy kindergarten and dog obedience classes provide important structure for the dogs, but it provides importantchances for properly socialization the puppy as well.

The Importance of Rewards

Rewards just may be the single most important motivator in dog training. Obedience training through the use of rewards and other positive reinforcements has long been recognized as the most effective method of reaching most dogs and getting the best possible results.

Making obedience training fun, and even making it a bit of a game, can be very important to keeping both the dog and the handler motivated and willing to learn. Incorporating a period of playtime at the beginning and end of every training session will make sure that every session begins and ends on a good note.

The most basic of all obedience commands is heeling, or walking with the handler on a loose lead. This is usually the first obedience behavior that is taught, and it is an easy one to teach through reward training. Begin by fitting the dog with a quality, properly fitted training lead and training collar. If you are unsure of how to fit the training collar, be sure to ask a dog trainer or the manager at the store where the equipment is purchased.

Start walking with the dog, always being cognizant of the dog's position relative to your own. If the dog begins to forge ahead, gently pull on the leash. This will engage the training collar and give the dog a gentle reminder to slow down. It may be necessary to apply greater pressure at first until the dog learns to accept the correction.

If the dog begins to fall behind, slow down and gently urge the dog forward. The use of a lure, or a favorite toy, can be very useful when teaching the dog to walk at your side. By keeping the lure at the desired position for the dog, he or she should quickly learn the desired location.

Always be sure to provide plenty of praise, treats, toys and other rewards when the dog does what is expected of him. Dogs learn best by positive reinforcement. Positive reinforcement means that when the animal does what the handler wants, it receives a reward, which can be anything from a pat on the head to a treat to a favorite toy. At the beginning of training, even the slightest attempts to please the owner should be rewarded.

Training by using reprimands and punishment is not nearly as effective as training by using rewards. Dogs can become discouraged and confused by excessive amounts of punishment and reprimands. Reprimands may be required from time to time, to correct potentially dangerous behaviors like chasing or biting, for instance, but reprimands should be short and directly attributed to the problem behavior at hand. After the immediate danger has passed, the training should continue with reward based training and positive reinforcement.

For instance, if you come home and your dog is chewing the furniture or other inappropriate item, immediately give the dog a sharp "No" or "Off" and take the item away. Then immediately give the dog one of his toys or other items that he is allowed to chew on, and praise the dog enthusiastically when he takes the toy and begins to chew it. This will teach the dog to associate chewing some items, like his toys, with praise, and chewing inappropriate items with reprimand.

It is very important for the dog to make these associations, since it is very hard to change negative associations once they have formed. It is always much easier to train proper obedience behaviors the first time than it is to go back and retrain a problem dog later on. That does not of course mean that retraining is impossible, it simply means that it is more difficult.

88

Teaching a puppy, or an older dog, to associate the behaviors you value, such as coming when called, sitting on command, walking at your side, chewing only on toys, etc. with happy, fun times is the basis of all successful dog training.

Chapter 9

Dog Training Issues

Refusing to Come When Called

Many dog owners fail to recognize the importance of having a dog that comes when called until there is a problem, such as the collar or leash breaking, or the dog tearing free to chase a person or another animal. These situations can be dangerous for the dog, the owner and other members of the community. In areas where there is a lot of vehicular traffic, the situation could even prove fatal to the dog.

Unfortunately, many well-meaning owners sabotage this important part of their dog's training by allowing it to run off leash and unattended. Whether the dog is allowed to run in the park, on the beach, or just play with other dogs, this teaches the dog that there are many fun things that do not involve its owner. In fact, from the dog's perspective at least, these fun times are often ruined by the appearance of the owner.

Look at things from the dog's perspective for a moment. You – the dog – are having a ton of fun running on the beach with all your doggy friends, and suddenly here comes this human to take you away from the fun. When you see the dog's point of view it is easy to see how the appearance of the owner, and the leash can be seen as a negative.

This negative perception causes many dogs to delay this outcome by refusing to come when they are called. From the dog's point of view, this makes perfect sense, since every minute of delay means another minute of romping on the beach or in the park. In other words, the dog has learned that the most rewarding thing to do is to ignore the calls of its owner. While this may seem like a good idea to the dog, it is definitely not a good thing from the owner's perspective.

For dogs who have not yet learned this type of avoidance behavior, it is best to prevent it from happening by supervising the dog at play, and making the time you spend with your dog as much, or more, fun, as the time it spends alone or with other dogs.

For dogs that have already learned the value of ignoring their owner, some retraining is definitely in order. It is vital that every dog respond to the "come here" command, for the safety of both humans and dogs alike.

One thing to avoid is following the "come here" command with unpleasant activities. Calling the dog, and then immediately giving him a bath, clipping his nails, taking him to the vet, etc. will quickly teach the dog that coming to the owner has negative consequences. It is best to ask the dog to come and then play with him, feed him, walk him or engage in other fun activities. If you do need to take your dog to the vet, bathe him, etc. be sure to allow some time to pass so the dog does not associate the "come here" command with the bad experience.

It is important to remember that dogs are constantly learning, whether a formal training session is in process or not. Your dog is always learning something from you, whether good or bad. It is therefore important to make every interaction with your dog a positive one.

When teaching the dog to come on command, it is vital that the dog be consistently rewarded every single time he does as the owner wants. A reward can be as simple as a pat on the head, a "good boy" or a scratch behind the ears. Of course, treat based rewards are appreciated as well, and many dogs are highly food motivated and respond quickly to this type of training. The key is to be consistent. The dog should get some kind of reward, whether it is praise, a toy, or a treat, every time he appears at the owner's side when called.

Training for Proper Dog Behavior

There are many reasons for teaching proper dog behavior, and teaching such behavior has many benefits for both the human and canine partners. Dog behavior training is vital to such life and death issues as preventing aggression, controlling dog on dog aggression problems and teaching dogs to interact properly with both their handlers and with other members of the family.

Understanding how dogs evolved, and how dogs interact with each other, is very important to understanding how to properly train your dog to be a devoted, loyal companion.

The original dogs were probably orphaned wolf pups adopted by early humans. These wild dogs probably learned to perform behaviors that their human protectors valued, such as guarding the cave or scaring off predators. In exchange for these valued behaviors, the humans probably provided their new companions with foods, protection and shelter.

That kind of relationship still exists today, of course, and dogs still can, and do, perform valuable jobs for their human benefactors. Those jobs include herding and guarding livestock, guarding property, guarding people, and finding game.

When planning a dog training program, it is important to know that dogs are pack animals. In wild dog societies, packs are formed, and each member of the pack quickly learns his or her place in the pecking order. Except in the event of death or injury to the alpha dog, the hierarchy never changes once it has been established. The lower dogs know not to challenge the alpha dog, and the alpha dog understand his place as leader of the pack.

All the other dogs in the pack look to the alpha dog for leadership, in important survival issues like finding food and avoiding larger predators. In order to properly train your dog and gain its respect, it is important for you to become the alpha dog.

That is because a dog that sees its owner as a superior leader will follow the commands the owner gives without question. Getting the respect of the dog is the most important step to proper dog training, and it will form the basis of all subsequent training.

The reasons for training a dog properly are many, especially in today's world. A well-mannered, obedient dog is a joy to be around, both for the owner and his or her family, and for people in the community at large. In addition, seeing a well-mannered dog sets people's mind at ease, especially with breeds of dog thought to be dangerous, such as Dobermans, rottweilers and pit bulls.

When training dogs and dealing with unwanted dog behaviors, it is important to understand the motivating factors behind those behaviors. For example, many dogs exhibit unwanted behaviors such as chewing and destroying furniture due to separation anxiety. Dealing with the sources of problem behaviors is an important first step toward eliminating those problem behaviors.

Many dogs exhibit unwanted behaviors as a result of stress in the animal's life, and its inability to cope with that stress. The goal of a good dog training program is to allow the dog to tolerate greater levels of stress without becoming a problem animal.

When dealing with dog behavior, it is important not to confuse human behavior with dog behavior. While there is a great temptation on the part of dog owners to see their dogs as almost human, in reality dogs and humans have very different motivations, and very different reactions to similar situations.

One trait that humans and dogs do share, however, is the need to form close social groups and strong bonds within those social groups. This bonding is important to both humans and dogs, but it has served vastly different ends as both species have evolved and changed over time.

Eliminating Biting Behaviors

Bringing home a new puppy is always an exciting time. Introducing the new puppy to the family should be fun for both yourself and your puppy. One of the first challenges, however, to the excitement of the new puppy, is curbing inappropriate puppy behaviors.

Preventing Biting and Mouthing

Biting and mouthing is a common activity for many young puppies and dogs. Puppies naturally bite and mouth each other when playing with siblings, and they extend this behavior to their human companions. While other puppies have thick skin, however, humans do not, so it is important to teach your puppy what is appropriate, and what is not, when it comes to using those sharp teeth.

The first part of training the puppy is to inhibit the biting reflex. Biting might be cute and harmless with a 5 pound puppy, but it is neither cute nor harmless when that dog has grown to adulthood. Therefore, puppies should be taught to control their bit before they reach the age of four months. Puppies normally learn to inhibit their bite from their mothers and their littermates,
96

but since they are taken away from their mothers so young, many never learn this important lesson. It is therefore up to the humans in the puppy's life to teach this lesson.

One great way to inhibit the biting reflex is to allow the puppy to play and socialize with other puppies and socialized older dogs. Puppies love to tumble, roll and play with each other, and when puppies play they bite each other constantly. This is the best way for puppies to learn to control themselves when they bite. If one puppy becomes too rough when playing, the rest of the group will punish him for that inappropriate behavior. Through this type of socialization, the puppy will learn to control his biting reflex.

Proper socialization has other benefits as well, including teaching the dog to not be fearful of other dogs, and to work off their excess energy. Puppies that are allowed to play with other puppies learn important socialization skills generally learn to become better members of their human family. Puppies that get less socialization can be more destructive, more hyperactive and exhibit other problem behaviors.

In addition, lack of socialization in puppies often causes fearful and aggressive behaviors to develop. Dogs often react aggressively to new situations, especially if they are not properly socialized. In order for a dog to become a member of the community as well as the household, it should be socialized to other people, especially children. Dogs make a distinction between their owners and other people, and between children and adults. It is important, therefore, to introduce the puppy to both children and adults.

The best time to socialize a puppy to young children is when it is still very young, generally when it is four months old or younger. One reason for this is that mothers of young children may be understandably reluctant to allow their children to approach large dogs or older puppies. This is especially true with large breed dogs, or with breeds of dogs that have a reputation for aggressive behavior.

Using Trust to Prevent Biting

Teaching your puppy to trust and respect you is a very effective way to prevent biting. Gaining the trust and respect of your dog is the basis for all dog training, and for correcting problem behaviors.

It is important to never hit or slap the puppy, either during training or any other time. Physical punishment is the surest way to erode the trust and respect that must form the basis of an effective training program. Reprimanding a dog will not stop him from biting – it will simply scare and confuse him.

Training a puppy not to bite is a vital part of any puppy training program. Biting behaviors that are not corrected will only get worse, and what seemed like harmless behavior in a puppy can quickly escalate to dangerous, destructive behavior in an adult dog.

Eliminating Bad Habits

Anyone who owns a dog or puppy will eventually run into the need to eliminate unwanted habits. While most dogs are eager to please their owners and smart enough to do what is asked of them, it is important for the owner to properly communicate just what constitutes acceptable and unacceptable behaviors.

Each type of unacceptable behavior requires its own specific cures, and in most cases the cures will need to be tailored to fit the specific personality of the dog. Every breed of dog has its own unique personality characteristics, and every individual within that breed has his or her own unique personality.

Whining, Howling and Excessive Barking

Let's start with one of the most frequently encountered problem behaviors in both dogs and puppies. While some barking and other vocalizing is perfectly normal, in many cases

99

barking, howling and whining can become problematic. This is particularly important for those living in apartment buildings, or in closely spaced homes. Fielding complaints about barking is not the best way for you and your dog to meet the neighbors.

Some tips of dealing with excessive whining, barking and howling include:

- ❖ If your puppy or dog is howling or whining while confined to its crate, immediately take it to its toilet area. Most puppies and dogs will whine when they need to do their business.

- ❖ It is important to teach a dog or a puppy to accept being alone. Many dogs suffer from separation anxiety, and these stressed dogs can exhibit all sorts of destructive and annoying behaviors. It is important to accustom the puppy to being left on its own, even when the owner is at home.

- ❖ Always strive to make the puppy or dog as comfortable as possible. Always attend to the physical and psychological needs of the dog by providing food, water and toys.

- ❖ If the dog is whining, check for obvious reasons first. Is the water dish empty? Is the dog showing signs of illness? Has his or her favorite toy rolled under the furniture? Is the temperature of the room too hot or too cold?

❖ Do not reward the puppy or dog for whining. If the dog whines when left alone, for instance, it would be a mistake to go to the dog every time it whines.

❖ After you have ensured that the dog's physical needs are being met, and that discomfort is not responsible for the whining, do not hesitate to reprimand the dog for inappropriate behavior.

Problem Chewing

Puppies naturally chew, and they tend to explore their world using their mouths and teeth. While chewing may be normal, however, it is not acceptable, and it is important to nip any chewing problems in the bud to prevent the chewing puppy from growing into a chewing dog.

Providing a variety of chew toys is important when teaching a puppy what is appropriate to chew and what is not. Providing a variety of attractive chew toys is a good way to keep the puppy entertained and to keep his teeth and gums exercised. Scented or flavored toys are great choices for most puppies.

The puppy should be encouraged to play with these chosen toys, and the puppy should be effusively praised every time he or she plays with or chews these toys.

Another great strategy is to encourage the puppy to get a toy every time he or she greets you. Every time the puppy greets you or a member of your family, teach him to get one of his toys.

It is also important to exercise good housekeeping techniques when training a puppy not to chew on inappropriate items. Keeping the area to which the puppy has access free and clean is important. Keeping items out of reach of the puppy will go a long way toward discouraging inappropriate chewing. Try to keep the puppy's area free of shoes, trash, and other items, and always make sure that the area has been properly puppy proofed.

If the puppy does pick up an inappropriate item like a shoe, distract the puppy and quickly replace the item with one of its toys. After the puppy has taken the toy, praise it for playing with and chewing that toy.

Try booby trapping items the dog should avoid by spraying them with bitter apple, Tabasco sauce or other nasty but non-toxic items.

Eliminating Problem Behaviors when Training Your Puppy

Unfortunately, eliminating problem behaviors is one thing that most dog owners eventually face. This article will focus on a few of the most commonly encountered behavior problems.

Problem #1 – Jumping up on people

One of the most frequently cited problems with dogs is that of jumping up on people. Unfortunately, this is one of those behaviors that are often inadvertently encouraged by well-meaning owners. After all, it is cute and adorable when that little 10 pound puppy jumps up on you, your family members and your friends. Many people reward this behavior on the part of a small puppy with kisses and treats.

This is a huge mistake, however, since that cute little puppy may soon become a full grown dog who could weigh well in excess of 100 pounds. Suddenly that cute jumping behavior is no longer quite so cute.

In addition to being annoying, jumping up on people can be dangerous as well. A large, heavy dog, jumping enthusiastically, can easily knock over a child or an older or handicapped adult. In today's litigious society, such an incident could easily make you, as the dog's owner, the subject of an unwanted lawsuit.

The time to teach a dog that jumping up on people is unacceptable is when he is still young and easy to handle. Retraining a dog that has been allowed to jump up on people can be difficult for the owner, and confusing for the dog.

When the puppy tries to jump on you or another member of your family, gently but firmly place the puppy's feet back on the floor. After the puppy is standing firmly on the floor, be sure to reward and praise him.

It is important for every member of the family, as well as frequently visiting friends, to understand this rule and follow it religiously. If one member of the family reprimands the dog for jumping and another praises him, the dog will be understandably confused. As with other dog training issues, consistency is the key to teaching the dog that jumping is always inappropriate.

When praising and rewarding the dog for staying down, it is important for the trainer to get down on the dog's level. Giving affection and praise at eye level with the puppy is a great way to reinforce the lesson.

Problem #2 – Pulling and tugging at the leash

Pulling on the leash is another problem trait that many puppies pick up. Unfortunately, this behavior is also one that is sometimes encouraged by well-meaning owners.

Playing games like tug of war with the leash, or even with a rope (that can look like the leash to the dog) can unwittingly encourage a problem behavior.

The use of a quality body harness can be a big help when training a puppy not to pull, or retraining a dog that has picked up the habit of pulling on the leash. Try training the puppy to accept the body harness the same way it accepts the regular buckle collar.

When walking with your dog, try using a lure or toy to encourage the dog to remain at your side. A training collar, when properly used, can also be a good training tool for a problem dog. When using a training collar or choke chain, however, it is very important to fit it correctly, and to use a size that is neither too big nor too small for your dog.

When walking with your puppy, it is important to keep the leash loose at all times. If the puppy begins to pull ahead, the handler should quickly change directions so that the puppy fast finds itself falling behind. It is important to reverse directions before the puppy has reached the end of the leash. The leash should stay loose except for the split second it takes the handler to reverse direction. It is important to use a quick tug, followed by an immediate slackening of the leash.

When training a puppy, it is important to never let the puppy pull you around. Training the puppy to walk properly while he or she is still small enough to handle is absolutely vital, especially when dealing with a large breed of dog. If your 150 pound Great Dane hasn't learned to walk properly while he or she is still a 20 pound puppy, chances are it never will.

It is important not to yank or pull on the puppy's neck when correcting him. A gentle, steady pressure will work much better than a hard yank. The best strategy is to use the least amount of pressure possible to achieve the desired result.

Problem #3 - Escaping and roaming the neighborhood

A responsible dog owner would never dream of allowing his or her dog to roam the neighborhood freely. Allowing a dog to roam on its own is irresponsible, dangerous (to the dog and the neighborhood), and probably even illegal. Most towns have ordinances which prohibit dogs from being allowed to roam around free, so you could be in legal trouble if your dog is found wandering the neighborhood unattended.

Of course sometimes that wandering dog is not the owner's idea, and many dogs perform amazing feats of escape when left on their own. The temptations for unattended dogs are many, including passing bicycles, joggers, children, cats and other dogs. It is much easier to prevent escapes than to recapture a loose dog, so let's talk about some preventative measures every dog owner can take.

Removing the motivation to escape is a big part of the solution. A bored dog is much more likely to spend his day plotting the great escape. A dog that is surrounded by everything he or she needs, like lots of toys, a soft bed, and plenty of fresh clean, water, is more likely to spend his or her day contentedly sleeping or playing with toys until the owner returns.

In addition, a dog with lots of pent up, unused energy is likely to try to escape. Try incorporating several vigorous play sessions with your dog into your daily routine. Make one of those play sessions right before you leave. If your dog has a chance to work of his or her energy, chances are he or she will sleep or relax much of the day.

Of course dealing with the dog is only half the problem. It is also important to make the property as escape proof as possible, through proper fencing and other measures. For dogs that dig, it may be necessary to extend the fence underground by placing metal stakes in the ground every few feet. For dogs that jump, it may be necessary to make the fence higher. And if none of these measures work, it may be necessary to confine the dog to the house when you are not at home.

Dog Training for Desired Behaviors

Teaching a dog proper behavior while it is young is very important. While playing and having fun with your new puppy or dog is certainly important, it is also important to teach your canine companion just what is expected – which behaviors are acceptable and which behaviors are not acceptable.

Teaching these lessons early, while the dog is still a puppy, is the best guarantee that these lessons will be learned and retained. Dogs learn quickly, and every interaction between human and dog is teaching the dog something. Making sure you are teaching the right lessons is up to you as the dog handler.

Proper training techniques are important for the protection of the dog as well as the protection of the family and the community at large. While dogs are loving, protecting members of the family in most cases, a poorly trained dog can be dangerous and destructive. Making sure your new addition is a pleasure to be around and not a menace is up to you as the owner.

The relationship between humans and dogs goes back for many thousands of years, and dogs have been domesticated longer than any other animals. Therefore, humans and dogs have developed a bond not shared by many other domesticated animals. This strong bond is very useful when training any dog.

All potential dog owners and would be dog trainers should understand how dog society works in the absence of humans. It is important to understand the pack hierarchy, and to use that hierarchy to your advantage as you train your dog. All pack animals have a lead animal, in the case of dogs it is the alpha dog. All other members of the pack look to the alpha dog for direction and guidance. The alpha dog in turn provides important leadership in hunting, fending off other predators, protecting territory and other vital survival skills. This pack arrangement is what has allowed wolves and wild dogs to be such successful predators, even as other large predators have been driven to extinction.

What all this means to you as the dog trainer is that you must set yourself up as the pack leader – the alpha dog if you will – in order to gain the respect and trust of your dog. If the dog does not recognize you as is superior and its leader, you will not get very far in your training program.

Respect is not something that can be forced. It is rather something that is earned through the interaction of human and dog. As the dog learns to respect and trust you, you will begin to make great strides in your training program. A training program based on mutual respect and trust is much more likely to succeed in the long run than one that is based on fear and intimidation.

A fearful dog is likely to at one point become a biting dog, and that is definitely one thing you do not want in your life. Rewarding the dog when he does the right thing, instead of punishing him for doing the wrong thing, is vitally important to the success of any training program.

Punishment only confuses and further frightens the dog, and it can set a training program back weeks if not months. It is important to give the dog the option to do the right thing or the wrong then, and to reward the dog when it makes the right decision. For instance, if the dog chases joggers, have a friend jog by while you hold the dog on the leash. If the dog attempts to chase the "jogger", sit him back down and start again. You are not punishing the wrong decision; you are simply providing the choice. When the dog sit calmly by your side, give him a treat and lots of praise. The dog will quickly learn that sitting is the right choice and chasing the jogger is the wrong choice.

Chapter 10

Advanced Dog Training Exercises

Coming when called is a vital skill that every dog must learn, both for its own safety and that of those around it. A disobedient dog that refuses to come when called could easily be hit by a car, get into a fight with another dog, or suffer a variety of other bad experiences. A well trained dog that comes when called can safely be taken out to play in the local park, at the beach, on the hiking trail, or anywhere else the owner and dog may wish to go.

Basic training to come when called is relatively easy and straightforward, and involves providing praise, treats and other perks when the dog does as his owner wants. After these basic come when called training exercises are mastered, there are a number of fun exercises that can be introduced to challenge the dog and pique its interest.

Making training into a fun game is one of the best ways to motivate dog and handler alike. It is easy for training sessions to become routine and boring, and it is important to keep them from degenerating into this state.

Before beginning any food based training exercise, it is important to make sure that the dog is properly motivated and ready to respond to treat based training. Testing the dog is simply a matter of taking a piece of his regular food and waving it in front of the dog's nose. If the dog shows great enthusiasm for the food, it is ready to start the training. If not, it is best to wait until the dog is in a more receptive mood.

The treats that work best for treat based training games like hide and seek are cut up quarter inch or smaller pieces of chicken, cheese or liver. In other words, something your dog will love. It is best to use very small pieces to avoid over-feeding the dog during the training sessions.

One great game for you and another family member or friend to play with your dog is simply back and forth recall. This is a great exercise for teaching your dog to come whenever it is called by a member of the family. Dogs often learn to only respond to one person, and this can be a problem when other people are watching the dog. That is one reason why professional dog trainers always insist on working with the owner as well as the dog. A well trained dog must learn to respond to whoever is in charge, not just the owner or usual handler.

In the back and forth recall game, two or more people stand approximately ten yards apart, in a safe place like a fenced in yard. One person calls the dog and asks him to sit and say until another person asks the dog to come. When the dog responds to the command to come, it is rewarded with a treat. Most dogs respond wonderfully to this exercise and love playing this game. When playing the back and forth recall game, it is important that only the person who called the dog be allowed to give the dog a treat.

After the dog has mastered the back and forth recall game, the humans in the game can start to spread further out, thus turning the back and forth recall game into a fun game of hide and seek. The hide and seek game starts with two or more people in the center room of the house. Every time they call the dog to come, they spread out further away from where they started. As the game continues, one person will be at one end of the house, while another may be at the opposite end. What makes the hide and seek game so much fun for the dog is that he must seek out the person to get the treat, instead of simply running up to a person in plain sight. This type of seeking behavior appeals to many of the dog's natural instincts. After all, dogs are naturally hunting animals, and seeking out food is second nature to them.

Keeping Your Dog Motivated

Keep the attention of a dog while training is not always easy. Dogs can be easily distracted, and it is important to not allow the training sessions to be sabotaged by boredom. Making training fun for the dog and the human alike is vital to creating a happy, well-adjusted and well trained dog.

Providing random positive stimuli during the day is a great way to keep the interest of the dog. Doing things the dog enjoys, like walking in the park, riding in the car, and playing with other dogs, is a great way to keep the dog's attention and reward him for small successes.

For instance, in order to reward the dog for coming to you, for instance, ask the dog to come to you, without giving any clues about a walk, a car ride, or other treats. After the dog has come to you and obediently sat down, attach the leash and start the reward. This can be either the aforementioned walk in the park, ride in the car, or anything else the dog likes to do.

Providing some kind of reward, whether a treat, a special outing or just a scratch behind the ears during each time the dog does something you want is a great way to keep your dog motivated. If the dog knows something great is going to happen every time he obeys your command, he will be motivated to please you every time.

Distraction Training

When training any dog, it is important to not let distractions disrupt the training. The dog must be taught to ignore distractions, such as other people, other dogs, other animals and loud noises, and focus on what is being taught. These types of distractions can even be used as rewards when training the dog to come when called.

For instance, if your dog enjoys playing with other dogs whether in a local dog park or with the neighbor's dogs, let him play freely with those other dogs. Then go into the park or yard and call your dog. When he comes to you, provide lots of praise, treats and other rewards, then immediately allow the dog to go back to playing with his friends. Repeat this several times and praise the dog each time he comes to you. The dog will quickly learn that coming to you means good things (treats and praise) and not bad ones (being taken away from the park).

If the dog does not master this particular type of training right away, try not to get discouraged. So called distraction training is one of the most difficult things to teach. Dogs are naturally socialanimals, and breaking away from the pack is one of the most difficult things you can ask your dog to do. Most dogs will be understandably reluctant to leave their canine companions, but it isimportant to persist.

Training the dog to come to you may require some creativity on your part at first. For instance, waving a favorite toy, or a lure, is a great way to get your dog's attention and put the focus back on you. If your dog has been clicker trained, a quick click can be a good motivator as well.

Once the dog begins to get the hang of coming when called, you can begin to reduce and eliminate the visual cues and focus on getting the dog to respond to your voice alone. It is important that the dog respond to voice commands alone, since you will not always have theavailability of a toy or other lure.

Chapter 11

More Dog or Puppy Training Issues and Exercises

Dealing with Separation Anxiety

Separation anxiety, also known in the dog training world as owner absent misbehavior, is one of the most frequently encountered problems in the world of dog training. Separation anxiety can manifest itself in many different ways, including chewing, destroying the owner's property, excessive barking, self-destructive behavior and inappropriate urination and defecation.

Dogs suffering from separation anxiety often whine, bark, cry, howl, dig, chew and scratch at the door the entire time their family members are away. Well-meaning owners often unwittingly encourage this misbehavior by rushing home to reassure the dog, but it is important for the well-being of both dog and owner that the dog learn to deal with extended periods of separation.

How the owner leaves the house can often contribute to separation anxiety issues. A long and drawn out period of farewell can make matters worse by making the dog feel even more isolated when the owner finally leaves. These long types of farewells can get the dog excited, and then leave him with lots of excess energy and no way to work it off. These excited, isolated dogs often work off their excess energy in the most destructive of ways, such as chewing up a favorite rug or piece of furniture.

Excess energy is often mistaken for separation anxiety, since results are often the same. If you think that excess amounts of energy may be the problem, try giving your dog more exercise to see if that eliminates the problem.

If separation anxiety is truly the problem, it is important to address the root causes of that anxiety. In order to prevent separation anxiety from occurring, it is important for the dog to feel happy, safe, secure and comfortable while the owner is away for the day. It is important, for instance, to give the dog plenty of things to keep it busy while you are away. This means providing it with lots of toys, such as balls or chew toys. A pet companion is often effective at relieving separation anxiety as well. Giving the dog a playmate, such as another dog or a cat, is a great way for busy pet parents and pets alike to cope with the stress of being left alone.

Setting aside scheduled play times, during which the pet is given your undivided attention, is another great way to alleviate boredom and separation anxiety. Playing with the dog, and providing it with sufficient attention and exercise is a proven way to avoid a stressed and anxious dog. A happy dog that has been well exercised and well-conditioned will generally sleep the day away happily and patiently wait for the return of its owner. It is important to schedule one of these daily play sessions before you leave the house each day. It is important to give the dog a few minutes to settle down after playtime before you leave.

For dogs that are already experiencing separation anxiety and associated misbehaviors, it is important to get him accustomed to your leaving gradually. Be sure to practice leaving and returning at irregular intervals, several times during the day. Doing so will get your dog accustomed to your departures and help him realize that you are not leaving him forever; Dogs that have been previously lost, or those that have been surrendered to shelters and readopted, often have the worst problems with separation anxiety. Part of treating this problem is teaching the dog that you're leaving is not permanent.

Preventing Unwanted Urination

Problems with inappropriate urination are some of the most commonly encountered by dog owners. As a matter of fact, inappropriate urination and defecation is the most frequently citedreason that owners surrender their animals to shelters.

Before you can address problems with inappropriate urination, it is important to understand the basis of the problem. There are several reasons why dogs lose control of their bladders, and it is important to know the root cause of the problem before it can be properly addressed.

Problem #1 – Excitement Urination

Dogs often urinate when they become overly excited, and dogs that are otherwise perfectly housebroken sometimes show their excitement by dribbling urine when greeting you excitedly. It is normal for some dogs to urinate when they get excited, and this can be a particular problemfor many older dogs.

A lot of excitement induced urination occurs in young puppies, and it is caused by a lack of bladder control. The puppy may not even know he is urinating, and punishment will simply confuse him. Becoming angry with the puppy will quickly cause excitement urination to morph into submissive urination, thus compounding the problem. As the puppy gets older and develops better bladder control, this type of excitement urination should disappear.

The best cure for excitement urination is prevention. Preventing your dog from becoming over excited is the best way to control this problem behavior. If your dog is excited by a particular stimulus or situation, it is important to repeatedly expose him to that situation until it no longer causes excessive excitement.

Problem #2 – Submissive Urination

Submissive urination is a natural part of pack behavior among animals like dogs and wolves. The submissive member of the pack shows his or her submissiveness by lowering itself and urinating. Since dogs are pack animals, they may show their submissiveness to their owner, who they regard as the pack leader, by exhibiting this submissive urination.

Dogs who exhibit submissive urination are usually showing their insecurity. Unsocial zed and previously abused dogs often exhibit submissive urination. These dogs need to be shown that there are more appropriate ways to express their submissive status, such as shaking hands or licking the owner's hand.

The best way to deal with submissive urination problems is often to ignore the urination. Trying to reassure the dog can give the mistaken impression that you approve of the behavior, while scolding the dog can make the submissive urination worse.

Correcting problems with submissive urination should be directed at building the dog's confidence and teaching him other ways to show his respect. Teaching the dog to lift his paw, sit on command, or similar obedience commands, is a great way to direct the dog's respect in a more appropriate direction.

Problems with urination are not always easy to deal with, but it is important to be consistent, and to always reward acceptable behavior on the part of the dog. When urination problems do occur, it is always a good idea to first rule out any medical conditions that could be causing those problems. Medical issues like bladder infections can be the root cause of problems with unwanted urination.

After any medical problems have been ruled out, it is important to determine what is causing the problem, and treat it appropriately. While it can be tempting to punish the dog for inappropriate elimination, doing so will only confuse and further intimidate him.

How to Train Your Dog Not to Chase People, Bicycles, and Joggers?

Dogs by nature are predatory animals, and all predatory animals share the motivation to chase fleeing objects. While this may be a natural instinct, it is not appropriate when those fleeing objects are joggers, bicyclists or the mailman.

Training the dog not to chase people and bicycles is an important thing to do, and it is best to start that training as early as possible. Starting when the dog is still small and non-threatening is important, particularly with breeds that grow very large, or with breeds that have a reputation for being very aggressive. Many people respond to being chased by a dog, especially a large dog, with understandable fear, and it is best for yourself and your dog that he be trained not to chase before he reaches a threatening size.

Some dogs are easier to train away from chasing than others. Breeds that have been used for hunting or herding often retain much more of their chasing instincts than other types of dogs, for instance.

No matter what breed of dog you are working with, however, it is important to not allow him off the leash until his chasing behavior has been curbed. Allowing an untrained dog off the leash is dangerous, irresponsible and illegal.

Before you expose your dog to a situation where he will want to chase someone or something, be sure to train him in a safe, controlled area like a fenced in yard. It is important for the dog to be able to focus and concentrate on you, and for him to understand what behavior you want. The dog must be given the opportunity to repeatedly perform the behavior you want while in this controlled setting.

The training session should be started indoors in the dog's home. The dog should be put on a leash and the owner and the dog should stand at one end of a hallway or a room. The owner then waves a tennis ball in front of the dog but does not allow him to touch it. After that, the tennis ball is rolled to the other end of the hallway or the room, and the command "Off" is used to tell the dog not to chase the ball. If the dog starts out after the ball, use the command "Off" once again and give a firm tug on the leash.

When doing this type of training, it is vital that the dog not be allowed to touch the ball. If he actually reaches the ball, he may think that "Off" means to get the ball. This exercise should be repeated several times, until the dog has learned the meaning of the "Off" command. When the dog responds correctly by not chasing the ball, he should be rewarded with a special treat.

After the dog seems to understand his new game, move to another room and try the same thing. Repeat the exercise in several rooms of the house, in the garage, etc. After the dog has seemingly mastered the game and learned the meaning of the "Off" command, you can work with him without the leash, but still only in a safe area like your own home or a fenced in yard. It may take some time for the dog to fully master control of his chasing instinct, and it is important not to rush the process, or to leave the dog off leash until you are sure he is fully trained.

To test the training in the real world, enlist the assistance of a friend to pose as a jogger. It is important that the dog does not see and recognize this person; he has to assume that it is a stranger in order for the test to be valid. Stand with the dog on his leash and have your friend jog by a couple of times while you do the "Off" exercise. If the dog does as he is asked, be sure to provide lots of praise and treats. If he starts after the "jogger", give a firm reminder by tugging on the leash.

Training the Shy or Fearful Puppy or Dog

With dogs as with people, some dogs and puppies are naturally more bold and daring than others. When you watch a group of puppies play, it will quickly become apparent which ones are bold and which ones are shy. Some of the puppies will hang back at the edge of the pack, perhaps fearful of angering the stronger dogs, while others will jump right into the fray and startjostling for control.

Working with a shy puppy or dog, or one that is fearful, presents its own special challenges. Of course bold, forceful dogs present challenges of their own, especially with control and leadership issues. Every type of puppy or dog has its own unique personality and its own uniquetraining challenges as a result.

One important reason to build confidence in a fearful dog is to prevent biting. High fear dogs often become biters to deal with their fear of new situations, and this type of fear response can be dangerous for you and your dog. It is important to teach the puppy or dog that new situations and new people are nothing to fear, and that they are not out to hurt him.

Signs of fear in both puppies and dogs include being afraid of strangers, being leery of new situations, and avoiding certain people or objects. A fearful puppy or dog may also snap or bite, especially when cornered.

If you recognize signs of fear in your dog or puppy, it is important to act quickly. Fear responses can quickly become ingrained in a dog, and once those fear memories are planted they can be difficult to erase. Properly socializing a young puppy is essential to making sure your dog is not fearful, and will not become a fear biter. Many puppies are raised as only dogs, but even these puppies should be given the opportunity to play with other puppies and with well socialized older dogs and friendly cats as well. The more novel situations the puppy encounters when he is young, the better he will be able to adapt to new situations as an adult dog.

Adapting to new and changing situations is a vital life skill that every puppy must learn. As you know, the world is constantly changing and adapting, and it is vital that both you and your four legged companion learn to take these changes in stride.

It is important for owners to not inadvertently reinforce or reward shy or fearful behaviors. For instance, when a puppy or dog shows fear, by whining, crying or hiding, it is only natural for the owner to go over and reassure the dog. This type of reassurance, however, can be misinterpreted by the animal as a sign of approval from the pack leader.

When the dog or puppy displays fearful or shy behavior, the best strategy is simply to ignore him. The dog must be able to learn on his own that there is nothing to fear. If left alone, a dog will often start to explore the fearful object on his own, thereby learning that the initial fear reaction was mistaken. The owner must allow the dog to explore things on his own, and not try to coddle or over protect him.

Another reason for fear reactions, particularly in older dogs, is past abuse or lack of proper socialization as puppies. The window for good puppy socialization is relatively short, and once this window has closed it can be difficult to teach a dog how to socialize with dogs and other animals. Likewise, a dog that has been abused probably has all sorts of negative associations, and it is up to a patient owner to work with the dog to replace those fear reactions with more appropriate responses.

When working with an older fearful dog, it is important not to try to rush the socialization and fear abatement process. It is best to simply allow the dog to explore things on his own, even if it means he spends a lot of time hiding from the perceived monster. Trying to force the dog to confront the things he fears will do more harm than good.

It is also important to address already ingrained fear based behaviors, such as biting, snapping and growling, whether they result from past abuse, a lack of socialization or a combination of factors. If the dog is frightened and reacts defensively to strangers, it is important to introduce him slowly. It is important to correct these potentially dangerous behaviors, however, and teach the dog that fears is no excuse for growling, snapping or biting. The best way to do this is to immediately reprimand and correct the dog when he bites, snaps or growls at anyone.

The dog should be generously rewarded the minute it stops displaying aggressive behavior. If you do find yourself having to reprimand your dog for displaying aggressive behaviors, it probably means you have tried to move him along too quickly. It is important to avoid threatening situations as much as possible until the dog has built up the confidence it takes to deal with those situations. If you think you have moved too fast, take a few steps back and let the dog regain his confidence.

Training Your Dog Not to Fear Loud Noises

Loud noises, such as fireworks, thunder and traffic, are one of the most frequently cited fears given by dog owners. It is natural for some dogs to be fearful of loud noises, but some dogs are so traumatized by thunder, fireworks and other loud noises that they are completely unable to function.

Dogs that display excessive fears or phobias such as these can be a danger to themselves and those around them. Dogs may manifest their fear in self-destructive ways, like slinking under the couch or the bed and getting stuck, for instance. They may also react in ways that are destructive to the home, such as urinating or defecating on the carpet, chewing up favorite items, or barking incessantly. These reactions are often worse when the owner is not at home.

One thing that is hard for many dog owners to understand is that soothing or stroking a dog that is displaying fear is exactly the wrong thing to do. While it is natural to try to calm a fearful dog, to the dog you are rewarding it for being afraid. The dog likes the sound of your voice, likes your petting, and concludes that he has done the right thing by acting afraid. This only makes a bad situation worse.

The best strategy when the dog displays fear when there is a thunderstorm or a fireworks display is to simply ignore the dog. It is of course important to watch the dog to make sure he does not hurt himself, but otherwise just ignore him and let him work through the fear on his own. When you go away, be sure to make sure there is nothing the dog can get stuck under, since fireworks or a thunderstorm can pop up at any time.

A dog that is severely afraid of thunderstorms and other load noises may need to be confined to a single room, or even a crate, for a period of time. After the dog feels safe in his "den", he may be able to deal with his fears a little better. It can be quite a struggle to teach a dog not to be afraid of thunderstorms, firecrackers and other such noises, but it is important that the
130

dog at least be able to control his fears without being destructive to himself or his environment.

Using Distraction

Much as magicians use sleight of hand to hide their tricks, so dog owners practice the art of distraction to take their dog's mind off of their fear. For instance, if your dog is afraid of thunderstorms and you know one is on the way, gather some of your dog's favorite toys and getready for the misdirection.

Of course, your dog will probably know the thunderstorm is on the way before you do. When you see your dog start to display fear, take a few of his favorite toys and try to get him to play. Very fearful dogs may be reluctant to play, but it is important to try nevertheless. Often a few treats can be a good distraction as well. Try buying one of those balls that you can fill with treatsor biscuits, and encourage your dog to chase it.

Try playing with your dog every time a thunderstorm is in the forecast. This can start to implant good memories, and these can sometimes replace the fear memories that caused the dog to beafraid of thunderstorms in the first place.

Desensitizing Your Dog's Fear

Desensitization is a highly effective way to deal with phobias and fears in humans, and it can be very effective for dogs and other animals as well. Desensitization involves introducing the dog to small amounts of whatever noises frighten him. For instance, if the dog is afraid of thunder, try tape recording your next thunderstorm and play it back slowly when the dog is relaxed. Reward the dog for not showing fear responses. If he does show fear responses, do not comfort or soothe him but just ignore him.

This kind of desensitization training can be remarkably effective for some dogs, but it will take lots of patience and hard work. Fears of thunder and fireworks are not always easy to cure.

Training Your Dog Not to Chase Cars

One of the most serious, and unfortunately most common, problem behaviors among dogs is that of chasing cars. Dogs must be trained as early as possible that chasing cars is not acceptable. That is because dogs that chase cars eventually become dogs that catch cars, and car plus dog always equals big trouble.

There are many reasons that dogs chase cars. For one thing, chasing moving objects is an ingrained, instinctual behavior that can never be completely removed. Chasing behaviors however can and should be controlled through a combination of good training and supervision.

Some dogs are more apt to chase cars, bikes, joggers, cats and other dogs than are others. Dogs that have a high prey drive, including breeds that have been bred for hunting, are particularly susceptible to the thrill of the chase. Herding breeds are also apt to chase cars, attempt to hurt the neighbor's children, or express other undesired traits of their breeding.

One reason that many dogs chase cars in particular is that they have learned to associate cars with good time and fun things. Most dogs love to ride in the car, and when they see a car they may try to chase it down for a ride.

No matter what your dog's motivation for chasing cars, however, it is important to curb this dangerous behavior as quickly as possible. Training the dog not to chase cars starts with teaching the dog the meaning of the "Off" command. The "Off" command is one of the basic tenets of obedience, and it must be mastered by every dog.

Teaching the dog to stay where he is, even if interesting, exciting things are happening elsewhere, is very important to all aspects of dog training. In the world of professional dog training, this is sometimes referred to as distraction training. Distraction training is very important, and it is applicable to teaching the dog not to chase cars.

Teaching this important lesson is not something you will be able to do on your own. You will need at least one other person – a volunteer who will slowly drive by and tempt your car with his bright, shiny object. You will stand with your dog on his leash as the volunteer drives by.

Having the volunteer drive your own car can provide an even greater temptation, since dogs are able to distinguish one car from another. If your car is the one that provides his rides, it is likely to be the most tempting object in the world.

When your friend drives by, either in your car or his, watch your dog's reaction carefully. If he begins to jump up or move away, repeat the "Off" command and quickly return your dog to the sitting position. If he remains where he is, be sure to give him lavish amounts of praise and perhaps a treat or two.

Repeat this process many times over the course of a few days. Once your dog is reliably remaining seated when your friend drives by, start lengthening the distance between yourself and your dog. A long, retractable leash works great for this process. Slowly lengthen the distance between you and your dog, while still making sure you have control.

Even after your dog is trained to not chase cars, however, it is important to not leave him out of the leash unsupervised. Leaving a dog unattended, except for within a properly and securely fenced in yard, is simply asking for trouble. Dogs are unpredictable, and it is always possible that the chase instinct could kick in at exactly the wrong moment. The best strategy is to confine the dog when you cannot supervise him.

Teaching Your Dog Not to Chew

Chewing is something that comes naturally to every dog. Every dog feels the instinctual need to sharpen its teeth and hone his biting skills. Chewing on the right things, like specially designed chew toys for instance, can even help the dog clean his teeth and remove plaque.

Even though chewing is natural and healthy, that does not mean that the dog should be given carte blanche and allowed to chew everything in sight. It is vital for every dog to learn the difference between the things it is OK to chew on, like toys and ropes, and the things that are off limits, such as carpets, shoes and other items.

When working with a new puppy, it is advisable to keep the puppy in a small, puppy proofed room for at least a few weeks. This is important not only to prevent chewing but to properly house train the puppy as well.

Older dogs should also be confined to a small area at first. Doing this allows the dog to slowly acquaint him or herself to the smells and sights of the new household.

When you set up this small, confined area, be sure to provide the puppy or dog with a few good quality chew toys to keep him entertained while you are not able to supervise him. Of course the dog should also be provided with a warm place to sleep and plenty of fresh clean water.

As the dog is slowly moved to larger and larger portions of the home, there may be more opportunities to chew inappropriate items. As the dog is given freer access to the home, it is important to keep any items that the dog or puppy should not chew, things like throw rugs, shoes, etc. up off of the floor. If you forget to move something and come home to find that the dog has chewed it, resist the urge to punish or yell at the dog. Instead, distract the dog with one of its favorite toys and remove the inappropriate item from its mouth.

The dog should then be provided with one of its favorite toys. Praise the dog extensively when it picks up and begins to chew its toy. This will help to teach the dog that it gets rewarded when it chews certain items, but not when it chews other items.

Teaching the dog what is appropriate to chew is very important, not only for the safety of yourexpensive furniture and rugs, but for the safety of the dog as well. Many dogs have chewed through dangerous items like extension cords and the like. This of course can injure the dog severely or even spark a fire.

Most dogs learn what to chew and what not to chew fairly quickly, but others are obviously going to be faster learners than others. Some dogs chew because they are bored, so providing the dog with lots of toys and solo activities is very important. It is also a good idea to schedule several play times every day, with one taking place right before you leave every day. If the dog isthoroughly tired after his or her play session, chances are he or she will sleep the day away.

Other dogs chew to exhibit separation anxiety. Many dogs become very nervous when their owners leave, and some dogs become concerned each time that the owner may never come back. This stress can cause the dog to exhibit all manners of destructive behavior, including chewing soiling the house. If separation anxiety is the root of the problem, the reasons for it must be addressed, and the dog assured that you will return.

This is best done by scheduling several trips in and out of the home every day, and staggering the times of those trips in and out. At first the trips can be only a few minutes, with the length slowly being extended as the dog's separation anxiety issues improve.

Training Your Puppy Not to Bite

Biting is one of those things that every puppy seems to do, and every puppy must be taught not to do. Like many behaviors, such as jumping up on people, biting and nipping can seem cute when the puppy is small, but much less so as he gets older, larger and stronger.

Left to their own devices, most puppies learn to control their biting reflex from their mothers and from their littermates. When the puppy becomes overenthusiastic, whether when nursing or playing, the mother dog, or the other puppies, will quickly issue a correction.

Unfortunately, this type of natural correction often does not occur, since many puppies are removed from their mothers when they are still quite young. It is therefore up to puppy's owner to take over this important process.

Socializing the puppy with other dogs and puppies is one of the best and most effective ways to teach the puppy the appropriate and non-appropriate way to bite, and to curb the biting response.

Many communities and pet stores sponsor puppy playtime and puppy kindergarten classes, and these classes can be great places for puppies to socialize with each other, and with other humans and animals as well. As the puppies play with each other, they will natural bite and nip each other. When one puppy becomes too rough or bites too hard, the other puppies will quickly respond by correcting it.

The best time for this socialization of the puppy to occur is when it is still young. It is vital that every dog be properly socialized, since a poorly socialized dog, or worse, one that is not socialized at all, can become dangerous and even neurotic. Most experts recommend that puppies be socialized before they have reached the age of 12 weeks, or three months.

Another reason for socializing the puppy early is that mothers of young children may be understandably reluctant to allow their young children to play with older or larger dogs. Since socializing the dog with other people is just as important as socializing it with other dogs, it is best to do it when the puppy is still young enough to be non-threatening to everyone.

It is important for the puppy to be exposed to a wide variety of different stimuli during the socialization process. The socialization process should include exposing the puppy to a wide variety of other animals, including other puppies, adult dogs, cats and other domestic animals. In addition, the puppy should be introduced to as wide a cross section of people as possible, including young children, older people, men, women and people from a variety of ethnic backgrounds.

While socialization is very important to providing the puppy with life lessons and preventing him from biting, it is not the only method of preventing unwanted biting and mouthing. Giving the puppy appropriate things to play with and bite is another good way to control inappropriate biting. Providing a variety of chew toys, ropes and other things the puppy can chew is important to preventing boredom, keeping his teeth polished and keeping him from chewing things he should not.

As with any training, it is important to be consistent when teaching the puppy not to bite. Every member of the family, as well as close friends, who may visit, should all be told that the puppy is to be discouraged from biting. If one person allows the puppy to chew on them while everyone else does not, the puppy will quickly become confused, and that can make the training process much more difficult than it has to be.

Building Confidence and Respect

The first thing that any successful animal trainer must do is win the confidence and respect of the animal to be trained. This important piece of advice definitely applies to the training of dogs. As social pack animals, dogs have a natural need to follow a strong leader. Setting yourself, the owner or handler, up as this leadership figure is the basis of any successful dog training program.

Until your dog has learned to trust and respect you, it will be difficult for any training program to be successful. Trust and respect are not things that can be forced, they must be earned through positive interaction with your four legged companion. After the dog has learned to trustand respect the owner, he or she may be amazed at how quickly the training session's progress.

Many new dog owners mistake love and affection for trust and respect. While it is of course good to shower your new dog or puppy with love and affection, it is also important to gain its confidence and respect. It is also important to not allow the puppy or dog to get away with everything it wants to. It is easy to let a dog take advantage of you, particularly when it is so cute and adorable. It is important, however, to set boundaries, and to establish acceptable andunacceptable behaviors.

Dogs actually appreciate these types of boundaries, since they are similar to the rules that the pack leader establishes in nature. Every dog in the pack knows what is expected of it, and knows its place in the pecking order. This kind of structured hierarchy allows the pack to function, hunt and survive as a single entity. Your dog is actually seeking this type of leadership. If he or she does not get leadership from you, he or she may be frightened or confused.

In addition, failure to gain the respect of the dog is very important to the well-being of both the human and the dog. A dog that lacks respect for its human owner can be dangerous as well as hard to live with. It is important to establish firm boundaries of good and bad behavior, and to consistently, effectively enforce those boundaries.

When dealing with a puppy, it is important to start gaining his respect and trust as soon as possible. Establishing an early bond is the best way to move the training and socialization process forward.

It is also important to make the initial training sessions short. Puppies have a notoriously short attention span, and even older untrained dogs may be unable to focus for more than 10 or 15 minutes at a time. It is best to make the lesson short and positive than to stretch it out and create a negative experience.

It is also a good idea to start and end each session with a period of play. Starting and ending the training sessions on a high note is important. Dogs make quick associations, and creating a positive association with obedience training will help to create a happy, healthy and well- adjusted dog. A happy dog will be easier to train, and more willing to please.

It is also important to keep the dog from becoming bored during the training sessions. Many dog owners make the mistake of drilling the dog on things like basic obedience skills, heeling, sitting, etc. While these obedience skills are important, and it is true that they will form the basis of more advanced skills, it is important to mix things up and make things fun for both yourself and your dog. The more variety you provide the better your dog, and you, will enjoy the training sessions.

CONCLUSION

The basis of training any animal is winning its trust, confidence and respect. True training cannot begin until the animal has accepted you as its leader respect you and entrusted you with his or her confidence.

The mistake many puppy owners make is mistaking love and affection for respect and confidence. While it is certainly important to love your new puppy, it is also very important that the puppy respect you and see you as his leader. Dogs are naturally pack animals, and every dog looks to the lead dog for advice and direction. Making you the pack leader is vital to the successof training any dog.

Failure to gain the respect of the dog can create a dog that is disobedient, out of control and even dangerous. Problem dogs are dangerous, whether they are created through bad breeding, owner ignorance or improper training. It is important to train the dog right from the start, since retraining a problem dog is much more difficult than training a puppy right the first time.

It is important for any new dog owner, whether working with a 12 week old puppy or a twelve year old dog, to immediately get the respect of the animal. That does not mean using rough or dangerous handling methods, but it does mean letting the dog know that you are in control of the situation. Dogs need structure in their lives, and they will not resent the owner taking control. As a matter of fact, the dog will appreciate your taking the role of trainer and coach as you begin your training session.

When working with the dog, it is important to keep the training sessions short at first. This is particularly important when working with a young puppy, since puppies tend to have much shorter attention spans than older dogs. Keeping the training sessions short, and fun, is essential for proper training.

Beginning training sessions should focus on the most basic commands. The heel command is one of the most basic, and one of the easiest to teach. Start by putting the dog or puppy in a properly fitted training collar. Be sure to follow the instructions for fitting and sizing the color to ensure that it works as intended.

Begin to walk and allow your dog to walk beside you. If the dog begins to pull, gently pull on the leash. This in turn will tighten the training collar and correct the dog. If the gentle pressure is ineffective, it may be necessary to slowly increase the pressure. Always be careful to not over- correct the dog. Using too much pressure could frighten the dog and cause it to strain more. I the opposite problem occur and the dog lags behind, the owner should gently encourage it until it is walking beside the owner.

Most dogs figure out the heeling concept fairly rapidly, and quickly figure out that they should walk beside their owners, neither lagging behind nor pulling ahead. Once the dog has mastered heeling at a moderate pace, the owner should slow his or her pace and allow the dog to adjust along with it. The owner should also speed up the pace and allow the dog to speed up as well. Finally, walking along and changing pace often will reinforce the lesson that the dog should always walk at the heel of the handler.

From heeling, the next step should be to halt on command. This halt command works well as an adjunct to heel. As you are walking, stop and watch your dog. Many dogs immediately realize that they are expected to stop when their handler does. Others may need the reminder of the leash and the training collar.

After the halt on command has been mastered, the handler should encourage the dog to sit on command as well. Once the dog has stopped, the handler gently pushes on the dog's hindquarters to encourage the sit. Usually, after this walk, halt, sit procedure has been done a few times; the dog will begin to sit on his own each time he stops. Of course, it is important to provide great praise, and perhaps even a treat, every time the dog does as he is expected.

In the conclusion, if you've followed all the guides in this book closely you should be ready to start training your dog with the most complex tricks and behaviors in a matter of weeks! Always remember to be patient and always use positive reinforcement to teach your dog.

Dogs that are abused or scared into obedience often don't have an actual understanding of the behaviors they learn and develop other behavioral problems that could make them a threat to you or your family. With a little patience and a lot of love you and your canine friend will be enjoying each other's company without worrying about behavioral issues in any time!